W. Somerset Maugham

W. SOMERSET MAUGHAM

by M. K. Naik

UNIVERSITY OF OKLAHOMA PRESS

NORMAN

By M. K. Naik
Jīvan-Venu (Bombay, 1953)

Library of Congress Catalog Card Number: 66–13430

Copyright 1966 by the University of Oklahoma Press, Publishing Division of the University. Composed and printed at Norman, Oklahoma, U.S.A., by the University of Oklahoma Press. First edition.

DEDICATED TO

B. H. Khardekar

Preface

.

THIS STUDY of Somerset Maugham attempts to examine the author's literary legacy from two points of view. First, it considers the whole of Maugham's work from 1896 to 1965. None of the very few analyses of Maugham, published so far, does this, for one reason or another. The investigations by R. H. Ward (G. Bles, 1937) and R. A. Cordell (Nelson, 1937) consider his writings up to 1937 only; the short pamphlet of thirty-six pages in the bibliographical series of supplements to *British Book News—Somerset Maugham*, by John Brophy (The British Council, 1952)—is manifestly limited in range and scope; *The Maugham Enigma*, edited by Klaus W. Jonas (Peter Owen, 1954), is an anthology of critiques; and Professor Karl J. Pfiffer's recent contribution, *W. Somerset Maugham—A Candid Portrait* (Gollancz, 1959), is more of an impressionistic summation than a systematic appraisal. Laurence Brander's *Somerset Maugham* (Oliver & Boyd, 1963) no doubt brings the story up-to-date, but as the subtitle indicates, it is only "a guide." My efforts, therefore, should go far towards satisfying the need for a comprehensive study of one of the most popular writers of the modern period.

Secondly, the point of view from which I have surveyed the work of Maugham is, it is hoped, a new one. The charge of cynicism leveled at Maugham has often been discussed by critics, but my study of the conflict between the two strains of

cynicism and humanitarianism in him is a new approach to
that writer's work.

I wish to express my gratitude to Principal V. K. Gokak,
who, time and again, scrutinized my work and made many helpful suggestions, and to Professor Armando Menezes, whose
stern blue pencil was an invaluable asset in preparing my manu-
script for publication.

Finally, I must also record my thanks to Mr. B. A. Olkar,
who introduced me to Maugham's works and encouraged me
to undertake a study of them, and to the staff of the University
of Oklahoma Press.

M. K. Naik

Karnatak University,
Dharwar, India
January, 1966

Contents

·

·

W. Somerset Maugham

CHAPTER ONE

The Conflict

.

A T THE HEART of the literary career of Somerset Maugham lies a baffling enigma: Here was a writer equipped at most points—a born storyteller, a shrewd observer of men and manners, and an able technician; blessed with a long and not uneventful life enriched by wide travel and experience; the author of about one hundred literary contributions which have won popular acclaim—and yet what did he leave, ultimately, by way of lasting creative achievement? Nothing except a "slender baggage," as he himself admitted with his characteristically ruthless honesty—"two or three plays and a dozen short stories,"[1] to which may be added a couple of novels for fair measure. How did this happen? The usual explanation, "Just for a handful of silver he left us," is too facile to be completely satisfying.

At the center of the Maugham-enigma lies a deep-seated conflict, a conflict between cynicism and humanitarianism, which is discernible in his early work, and the growth and influence of which can be traced through his career to his final achievement.

It is necessary, at the outset, to define the terms "cynicism" and "humanitarianism." A philosophical analysis of the two concepts is not proposed, for as a matter of fact, neither of these

[1] A Writer's Notebook, 338.

concepts can strictly be called a "philosophy of life." The phrase "philosophy of life" denotes an organized and comprehensive system of thought, whereas cynicism (using the word not in its ancient, but modern sense) and humanitarianism are but attitudes towards life and will be treated as such. The connotation of these two terms will therefore be determined by the meaning and significance ascribed to them in modern English and modern literary criticism.

I

Cynicism, as we understand it today, may be regarded, in the first place, as a tendency to disbelieve in the sincerity or goodness of human motives and actions, and secondly, as a habit of expressing this disbelief by sneers, sarcasms, and captious fault-finding, arising from a lack of sympathy for erring humanity on one hand and from a feeling of superiority on the other. A disposition to look upon human life and morals with a frigid indifference, originating out of the conviction that "all is vanity," appears to be another mark of cynicism—hence the absence of warmth in the cynic's outlook upon men and things. Being a self-centered individualist, the cynic is interested in men, only so far as they satisfy his curiosity and provide food for his cynicisms. The varied spectacle of life, the joys and sufferings of men, the heights to which human nature can rise and the depths to which it can sink, and the drama of crime and punishment do not *move* him, though they may interest him and even rouse his curiosity.

Cynicism, from the psychological point of view may sometimes be the defense mechanism employed by the sensitive mind to protect its own sensitivity. Sometimes, a mind which is keenly sensitive suffers sorely due to its emotionality, and hence tries, consciously or unconsciously, to combat, supress, or hide its innate sensitivity. The sentimentalist may, thus, by choice

4

try to turn cynical, and may succeed, at least partially, in the attempt. As Arnold Bennett observes, "Every artist is tempted to sentimentalise or to be cynical—practically the same thing."[2] Many cynics, because of early frustration and suffering, developed an embittered, warped, and cold outlook upon life and men.

It may not, perhaps, be possible to detect all these strands in the web of cynicism in a single mind. There may, indeed, be subtle shades of cynicism, leading to the thing itself in its most complete form. Thus, the attitude of mind, which loves sneering and faultfinding, attended by a lack of reverence and pity, though not entertaining any radical disbelief in the sincerity of human motives, appears to touch, very closely, the borderland of cynicism. Thus, Aristophanes, scoffing at contemporary Greek literature, politics, and religion, appears at least in some places in his work to stand almost on the brink of the cynical attitude. It is only his lyricism and his respect for the old Greek values, which he seeks to defend by scoffing at the new, that save him from falling over.

Then, there is also a cynicism which has its origin solely in a defense reaction to emotionality. The mind, if thus affected, cannot remain loyal to cynicism for long. Byron's mind is a case in point. The unhappy circumstances of his childhood, his clubfoot and the humiliation to which it constantly put him, and his early disappointment in love—all these caused his mind, endowed with keen sensibility, to despise itself and its sensitiveness. The proud adolescent soon grew a thick skin, and the result, ultimately, was the unabashed and almost brutal cynicism of parts of *Don Juan*, though moods of tenderness continued, to the end, to break through the cynical hide. Thackeray is another illustration of this pseudo-cynicism. Although frequently accused of cynicism, Thackeray was, in reality, "the great senti-

2 *Author's Craft*, 65.

mentalist" as Oscar Wilde[3] called him. Thus, the cynical asides of *Vanity Fair* dissolve in the lush sentimentality of *The New-comes.*

Neither of these two types of mind can be called strictly "cynical." Of Cynicism in its complete form, of that type of mind, where the different strands of cynicism as analyzed above meet, the congenitally sentimental English can, perhaps, hardly present an example. To illustrate cynicism proper, one must turn to their neighbors across the channel, who have a more analytical bent of mind.[4] Rochefoucauld's *Maxims* (1665) are a fine example of cynicism in its complete form.[5] They reveal that type of mind which is suspicious of all human motives, which shows this disbelief by constant sneering, which looks upon life and morals with frigid indifference, and in the making of which, early frustration and disappointment have played a definite part.

The Maxims, a collection of about five hundred detached and brief observations on men and morals, are the work of a man whose political life had been ruined by an unlucky liaison, and who had endured prison and exile in playing the political game. *The Maxims* thus reveal an embittered materialist, frigid-

[3] *The Decay of Lying, Selected Works* (ed. by R. Aldington), 52.

[4] "Why the French should be so much pleasanter as cynics than other people is mysterious, except of course that cynicism, to be tolerable, must have grace and wit; apart from these, it's just bad manners. An English cynic is a man with a general grievance. A German cynic is a sort of a wild bore. A Scandinavian cynic is a pestilence. An American jumps around too much to make a cynic and a Russian's state of mind is not constant enough."—John Galsworthy, *The End of the Chapter*, 559.

[5] Swift has frequently been accused of cynicism. Indeed, the connection between him and Rochefaucauld can be pointed out by referring to a letter to Pope in which Swift owns the French writer as his "favourite" because, he says, "I have found my whole character in him." But Swift must be absolved of the charge of cynicism, because he is incapable of the frigid indifference to life and morals, which is a fundamental element in cynicism. Moreover, even in the lowest depths of his misanthropy Swift holds fast to certain values, as for example, his faith in "True Reason," which he attributes to horses, though not to men, in the last part of *Gulliver's Travels*.

ly contemptuous of men and morals. The general character of
The Maxims is indicated by the remark which is prefixed as a
motto to the fourth edition: "Our virtues are most commonly
mere vices in disguise." *The Maxims* themselves are only varia-
tions of this theme. All human motives are suspect to Rochefoucauld: ". . . We should be ashamed of our best actions, if the
world were witness to the motives which produced them." He
has no pity for human misery, for "There are in affliction several
kinds of hypocrisy: we weep to acquire the reputation of being
tender; we weep, in order to be pitied; we weep that we may be
wept over; we even weep, to avoid the scandal of not weeping."

This is how the French cynic regards benevolence: "Everyone takes pleasure in returning small obligations; many go so
far as to acknowledge moderate ones, but there is hardly any
one who does not repay great obligations with ingratitude." Of
idealism he later says, "The shame that arises from the praise
which [we] do not deserve often makes us do things which we
should never otherwise have attempted." His sneer at love is
characteristic: "To fall in love is much easier than to get rid of
it." But his bête noire is vanity, which according to him is the
mainspring of all human actions.

There is, obviously, much truth in Rochefoucauld's judgment of men and morals. Yet it need hardly be pointed out how
warped and extremist is his world view or how restricted and
distorted his portrait of humanity. One has only to turn from
the cold cynicism of Rochefoucauld to the sterling common
sense of La Bruyere's[6] aphorisms and to the deep sympathy and
profound belief in the simple goodness of the human heart, in
Vauvenargues'[7] maxims, in order to understand the limitations
of Rochefoucauld's *Weltanschauung*.

[6] *Caracteres de Theophraste* (1688).
[7] *Introduction a la connaissance de l'esprit humain* with "Reflexions" and
"Maximes" appended (1746).

7

Before concluding this examination of cynicism, one important problem may be posed: What effect does an artist's cynicism have on his creative faculty? Now, it is obvious that if the cynical artist is armed with sharp sneers and faultfinding and probes deep and mercilessly into human motives, he will, paradoxically enough perform a signal service to humanity, to which he will be indifferent. Since the cynic's searchlight is brought to bear upon many a chink in the human armor, exposing many charlatans, his work is most precious. Yet it must, in the ultimate analysis, appear to be wholly destructive. In that higher region of creative art, where the full significance of human life is revealed through the synthesizing power of imagination and emotion, sympathy, understanding and deep ratiocination, cynicism prevents the artist from fully realizing his creative potentiality. With all its brilliance and arresting quality, the cynic's vision of life remains hopelessly lopsided and woefully inadequate. The greatest artists have had their cynical moods, but their greatness lies in the fact that they were ultimately able to triumph over these moods and to develop an outlook whereby they could see life "steadily" and see it "whole." A persistently cynical outlook on life usually lessens an artist's creative stature by shutting him out from a vast and fertile tract of experience, from the rich and limitless universe of emotion and imagination, sympathy, and understanding. Cynicism clips the wings of the soul.

II

In order to understand all the implications of the term "humanitarianism," it is necessary to consider the general principles of the humanitarian creed, of which a very succinct analysis has been made by H. S. Salt.[8] Humanitarianism, as he points out, is not only a principle but a "faith . . .—the ethical

[8] *Encyclopaedia of Religion and Ethics*, Vol. 6, pp. 836–40.

belief of the future—the faith of universal kinship." It is the deliberate and systematic study of humane principles, and the attempt to show that humaneness is an integral part, if not the actual basis, of morals. It includes and comprehends both philanthropy—love of mankind—and zoöfily—kindness to animals.

Humanitarianism is based upon the acceptance of compassion as a moral force and upon the conviction, with Schopenhauer, that "compassion is an undeniable fact of human consciousness, residing in human nature itself." This compassion is universal sympathy with all sentient beings, such sympathy being duly proportioned to the sensibility of its object. Moreover, this sympathy, before it can be put to practical service, must be tested by experience and reason. Thus, the function of humanitarianism is to reconcile the ideal with reality, to unite compassion with judgment, and to discover not only how we feel or ought to feel towards our fellow beings, but also to what extent and with what limitations we can put these feelings into practice. Again, it is not merely a prohibitive, negative, and ascetic view of life that prompts us to desist from certain practices in which we might otherwise take pleasure; on the contrary, it adds immensely to the beauty and happiness of life by fostering a sympathy for the whole world of animate beings.

The term "humanitarianism," as applied to literature and literary criticism, has obvious affinities to the principles of the humanitarian creed. Humanitarianism may thus denote, in the first place, a compassion and sympathy for the afflictions of all sentient beings. As contrasted with the cynic, therefore, the humanitarian writer does not indulge in sneering or captious faultfinding at the expense of erring humanity. On the contrary, he is more apt to defend and pity the victim rather than scoff at or condemn him.

Secondly, humanitarianism also implies the desire and

power to understand others and their problems. To sympathize fully with another person requires sufficient imagination to mentally project one's self into the other's situation and see things from his point of view. This means that the humanitarian must abandon his self-centeredness. He cannot afford to be indifferent to life and morals as the cynic always is; in fact, he is deeply committed and must share the passion and the pain of humanity.

Thirdly, humanitarianism is also incompatible with "disbelief in the sincerity or goodness of human motives and actions," for compassion, understanding, and love for man would be impossible in the humanitarian without a firm belief in the goodness of human nature. In fact, the humanitarian is even apt to see "the soul of good in things evil," and champion the cause of the "fallen," the so-called enemies of society, whom he is not prepared to give up as altogether lost.

The humanitarian strain may take several forms in literature: It may appear in the form of a deep sense of pity and regard for the lower animals as is revealed in Cowper, who was "the friend of every animal that breathed"; in Blake, who believed that "A Robin red-breast in a cage puts all Heaven in a rage"; in Burns, who knew his animals as intimately as if they belonged to his circle of friends; in Sterne, whose Uncle Toby would not hurt a fly, for "This world surely is wide enough to hold both thee and me"; and in Hardy, for whom the "Blinded Bird" that sang zestfully forgetting the indignity was a symbol of divine charity.

On the human plane several manifestations of humanitarian compassion are observable. One may take the form of sympathy for the victims of an unjust political regime or of an oppressive social order, as in Dickens and Galsworthy, or of compassion for the fallen and the disgraced, the mentally warped and diseased, and even for the criminals and so-called enemies of society, as in Dostoevski. Another kind may appear as a deep sense of pity for the fate-persecuted human condition, as in Hardy, who, significantly enough, places loving kindness even above love, or as an all-embracing catholicity of sympathy, as in Shakespeare, for whom even Caliban is not a hopelessly lost soul.

The question, what effect do humanitarian tendencies in a writer have on his creative faculty, almost seems to answer itself: Compassion and sympathy, love and understanding of humanity, a firm faith in the innate goodness of human nature —these qualities seem to give to the humanitarian writer's work a deep human warmth, a catholicity of outlook, a nearness to life, and an insight into the human heart.

There are, of course, pitfalls in the path of the humanitarian writer, the most obvious and dangerous being that of sentimentalism—a pitfall that Dickens could not always avoid. At his worst, the morbidly sentimental humanitarian is as apt to give a one-sided and extremist rendering of life as is the cynic in his own way. But, with a stern sense of balance, as in Galsworthy, or of comprehensiveness, as in Shakespeare, these dangers can be effectively overcome.

Another trap, that of emotion and compassion leading the humanitarian writer off on tangents and thus making his work suffer as art on the formal or technical side, is not of equally great import. In fact, neither Shakespeare, nor Dickens, nor Dostoevski can be called a perfect artist. Shylock seems to abuse Shakespeare's sympathy for him and threatens (at least for the modern reader) to snap the web of romantic comedy in *The Merchant of Venice*. The play suffers on the formal side, but gains immeasurably in rich overtones. The human warmth and vividness of portraiture of Dickens' sprawling narratives would perhaps have been impossible if his novels had been put in cast-iron form. In Dostoevski, superb psychological analysis sits cheek by jowl with crude incidents, fit for a cheap detective tale, and dreary theological discussion with warm human portraiture. Yet, this does not prevent his work from attaining true greatness.

It is remarkable, on the other hand, how the presence of a rich humanitarian strain in the work of these writers has given their literature human appeal and insight into life—humanitarianism balances the effects of self-centeredness and mistrust.

In Somerset Maugham there seemed to be a blend of these two attitudes toward life—cynicism and humanitarianism—a blend that resulted in a conflict which affected the author's stature as a creative artist.[9]

[9] A fuller discussion of the terms "cynicism" and "Humanitarianism" is given in Appendix A.

CHAPTER TWO

The Man Himself

·

I HAVE PUT the whole of my life into my books," observes Maugham in *The Summing Up*.[1] Much light could be thrown upon the conflict between the author's cynicism and humanitarianism by inquiring into his life and the nature of the personality which shaped his work. That such an investigation is likely to be fruitful is clear from Maugham's own dictum: "A work of art is an arrangement which the author makes of the facts of his experience with the idiosyncrasies of his own personality."[2]

Although he is of Irish descent, William Somerset Maugham was born in Paris on January 25, 1874, where his father, Robert Ormond Maugham, was solicitor to the British Embassy. Maugham's maternal grandmother had settled in France after her husband's death, and it is interesting to note that she "wrote novels in French *Pour Jeunes filles.*"[3]

Maugham's early childhood was spent in France. In fact, the boy spoke French before he spoke English, and he attended a French school. The only lessons in English which he received at this time were from the English clergyman at the church attached to the Embassy, whose method of teaching English was to have his pupil read aloud police-court news in *The*

1 Page 6.
2 Page 2.
3 *The Summing Up*, 11.

Standard—a fact of which much could be made by an adverse critic dwelling upon Maugham's preoccupation with themes of adultery and scandal.

Maugham's mother died of consumption when he was eight. She was a beautiful woman, ". . . very small, with large brown eyes and hair of a rich reddish gold, exquisite features and a lovely skin."[4] The memory of her beauty and her love for him, who was her youngest son, seems to have haunted Maugham; and some of the tenderest lines in the otherwise tight-lipped *Summing Up* are those which refer to her: "When I was a small boy and unhappy, I used to dream night after night that my life at school was all a dream and that I should wake to find myself at home again with my mother. Her death was a wound that fifty years have not entirely healed."[5] He lost his father two years later.

The orphaned Maugham was sent to live with his uncle, the Reverend Henry MacDonald Maugham, vicar of Whitstable, Kent. Life at the vicarage was not exactly pleasant for the boy, and Maugham drew unfavorable pictures of it in *Cakes and Ale* and *Of Human Bondage*. The uncle is portrayed as a weak, indolent man, and the aunt, a childless woman, as fragile and equally insipid. They were apparently only too eager to do their best for the nephew, but good intentions could not replace genuine love. The boy was thus starved of affection when he needed it most.

Maugham had more than one problem to which he had to adjust. Weak and undersized, he had the seeds of consumption in his lungs—probably a hereditary disposition passed to him by his mother—and was also burdened with a marked stammer. His life at the preparatory school must have been, at times, an almost unbearable ordeal. What he suffered there is probably

[4] *Ibid.*, 11.
[5] *Ibid.*, 211.

suggested by the touching picture of Philip Carey's school days in *Of Human Bondage*. The description of how Philip's club-foot caused him to become an exceedingly sensitive and self-conscious boy, indulging in self-pity, and how it slowly rendered him a completely self-centered and morbid adolescent reveals much about Maugham's own childhood and adolescence.

Unable to feel at home either with his uncle or in the school at Canterbury, the lonely youth longed for freedom. He persuaded his uncle to let him go to Germany for one year. The idea was enthusiastically supported by his aunt, who was of German descent. The German interlude proved to be a pleasant experience for the growing boy. As Maugham put it in *The Summing Up*, "when I came back from Germany, aged eighteen . . . I had been happier than ever before. I had for the first time tasted freedom."[6]

Young Maugham had, by now, very decided views of his own about his future. His uncle wanted him to become an Anglican clergyman, but the thought of going to Cambridge and being subjected once more to restraint was irksome, especially since he had experienced freedom. Finally, after working for some time in a chartered accountant's office, he entered Saint Thomas' Hospital as a medical student in 1892. The medical profession did not really interest Maugham for his ambition was to become a writer, but as a medical student, he had the opportunity to live in London and gain the experience of life that he desired. His work in the out-patients ward was particularly rewarding. "For here I was," he tells us, "in contact with what I most wanted, life in the raw. In those three years I must have witnessed pretty well every emotion of which man is capable. It appealed to my dramatic instinct. It excited the novelist in me."[7]

[6] *Ibid.*, 41.
[7] *Ibid.*, 42.

Maugham's first novel, *Liza of Lambeth* (1897), was based upon what he had observed in the slums of Lambeth, where his work as a medical student took him. The success of the novel encouraged him to abandon medicine for literature, though in the meanwhile he had qualified as a doctor. He now drew up an ambitious plan of travel as part of his education for authorship: To go to Spain to learn Spanish, to go to Rome to master Italian, to follow that up with a journey to Greece, where he intended to learn the vernacular as an approach to ancient Greek, and, finally, to go to Cairo to learn Arabic. He soon found, however, that he would have to postpone his education "to a more convenient moment,"[8] because the next ten years—from 1897 to 1907—were indeed most inconvenient. The success of *Liza* had been a pleasant surprise, but ten years of repeated failures of his plays and novels were a most unpleasant experience. During these years, spent mostly in Paris, Maugham wrote and nearly starved.

At last, in 1907, his luck turned, when *Lady Frederick* was produced at the Court Theatre. A few months later he had four plays running at once, a fact which was suitably commented upon by *Punch* in a cartoon in which Shakespeare was shown biting his fingers while standing in front of the boards which advertised Maugham's plays. Ada Leverson has drawn an interesting portrait of the Maugham of this period in her novel, *The Limit* (1914), where Maugham appears as Hereford Vaughan, a young dramatist who is the rage of the day.

Hereford was to those who did not know him before, an agreeable surprise. Heaven knows what exactly people expected of him. Perhaps the men feared 'side' and the women that he would be overpowering after so many triumphs but he was merely a rather pale, dark and rather handsome young man. He behaved like anybody else, except that perhaps his manner

8 *Ibid.*, 68.

was a little quieter than the average. Unless one was very observant (which one is not) or unless one listened to what he said, he did not at first appear too alarmingly clever. He had one or two characteristics which must have at times led to misunderstandings. One was that whatever or whoever he looked at, his dark, opaque eyes were so full of vivid expression that women often mistook for admiration what was often merely observation. For instance, when he glanced at Lady Walmer she at once became quite confused, and intensely flattered, nearly blushed and asked him to dinner. While, if she had but known, behind that dark glance was merely the thought, "so that is the woman that Royalty . . . what extraordinary taste." Vaughan always used exaggerated modesty as an armour against envy, for envy, as a rule, is of success rather than of merit.[9]

Having achieved success as a playwright, Maugham determined, as he stated it, "to devote the rest of my life to playwriting." But at the very height of his success as a writer of gay comedies, he experienced an urge to unburden himself of all the pain of his childhood and adolescent experiences; subsequently, he turned his back upon the theater and wrote *Of Human Bondage* (1915), a novel which is largely autobiographical. Then World War I broke out. "A chapter of my life had finished," writes Maugham, "A new chapter began."[10] He enlisted with a Red Cross ambulance unit and was sent to France. Later, he was transferred to the intelligence department, and these experiences are recorded in parts of *Ashenden or The British Agent* (1928).

Maugham married Gwendolen Syrie Bernardo in 1915. A daughter was born of the marriage, but Mrs. Maugham obtained a divorce in 1927, and Maugham did not remarry.

His health had suffered while doing intelligence work in Switzerland, and he decided to travel. "I wanted," he observes,

9 Pages 52–53.
10 *The Summing Up*, 131–32.

17

"to recover my peace of mind—shattered through my own foolishness and vanity by occurrences upon which I need not dwell, and so made up my mind to go to the South Seas."[11] There was a professional reason also: gathering material for a novel on the life of Paul Gauguin, which later appeared under the title *The Moon and Sixpence* (1919).

How deeply this journey to the South Seas affected Maugham must be told in his own words: "I went looking for beauty and romance and glad to put a great ocean between me and the trouble that harassed me. I found beauty and romance, but I found also something I had never expected. I found a new self."[12] The writer in Maugham discovered in this remote corner of the world a mine of human character—human character in its elements, with the mask of culture torn from its face. He utilized this vast source of material to good purpose in many of his short stories.

On his return Maugham had to spend two years in a sanatorium in Scotland as a tuberculosis patient. Here, too, he struck a rich lode of human nature—human nature absorbingly interesting because it was severally twisted and strengthened or weakened by disease, forced leisure, and aloofness from the world. "I think," he wrote, "I learnt a good deal about human nature in that sanatorium that otherwise I should never have known."[13] One of the best of Maugham's short stories, viz., "Sanatorium," owes it origin to these experiences.

When he recovered from his illness, Maugham became an indefatigable traveler, journeying through China, Malaya, Burma, India, and many other countries.

I journeyed over a dozen seas, in liners, in tramps, in schooners, I went by train, by car, by chair, on foot, or on horse-

[11] *Ibid.*, 134.
[12] *Ibid.*, 134.
[13] *Ibid.*, 138.

back. . . . I became aware of the specific benefit I was capable of getting from travel; before, it had been only an instinctive feeling. This was freedom of the spirit on the one hand, and on the other, the collection of all manner of persons who might serve my purposes.[14]

He ceased to travel only when, as he says, he felt that travel could give him nothing more.

He then settled down in Cape Ferrat, Alps Maritimes, France, in his famous Villa Mauresque, which he had bought in 1928. During World War II, Maugham again served in the intelligence department. When France capitulated, he had to flee to England, leaving behind his home and all his belongings. From there, he traveled to the United States under a special arrangement with the British government. He remained there for six years before returning to his home in France in 1946.

In 1949, Maugham declared that he was officially retiring as a professional writer, though he published two books of essays after that—*The Vagrant Mood* (1952) and *Points of View* (1958), the latter being, according to him, "the last book I will ever publish." Today, Maugham is one of the most widely read of modern English writers. He was awarded the Order of Merit in 1953.

Throughout *The Summing Up*, Maugham speaks of "the pattern of life" which he wanted to design for himself. Authorship, we are told, was only one part of the pattern.

It did not seem to me enough only to be a writer. The pattern I had designed for myself insisted that I should take the utmost part I could in the affair of being a man. I desired to feel the common pains and enjoy the common pleasures that are part of the human lot. I saw no reason to subordinate the claims of sense to the tempting lure of the spirit and I was determined to get whatever fulfilment I could out of social intercourse and

14 *Ibid.*, 138.

human relations, out of food, drink and fornication, luxury, sport, travel, and as Henry James says whatever. But it was an effort and I have always returned to my books and my own company with relief.[15]

And again:

For my own satisfaction, for my amusement and to gratify what feels to me like an organic need, I have shaped my life in accordance with a certain design, with a beginning, a middle and an end . . . . We are the product of our natures and our environment. I have not made the pattern that I thought best, or even the pattern I should have liked to make, but merely that which seemed feasible. There are better patterns than mine.[16]

But Maugham seems, on the whole, to have been satisfied with his own pattern.

In the light of this sketch of Maugham's life and career, the different strands in the author's mental make-up become more apparent. The whole picture of Maugham's literary personality may be summed up as the story of a sensitive soul— shy and reticent—starved of affection, warped by a physical disability and by an orphaned and unhappy childhood—a sensitive soul recoiling under early rebuffs, withdrawing into its shell, and slowly becoming hard, and at times bitter, and ultimately learning to view the spectacle of pain and pleasure in life with amused tolerance and almost cynical indifference.

This portraiture is corroborated by Maugham's clear-sighted self-analysis in *The Summing Up*: "I had many disabilities," he says, referring to his early life, and adds that:

I was small; I had endurance but little physical strength; I stammered; I was shy; I had poor health. I had no facility for games, which play so great a part in the normal life of Englishmen; and I had, whether from any of these reasons or from

15 Page 61.
16 *The Summing Up*, 200–201.

nature I do not know, an instinctive shrinking from my fellow-men that has made it difficult for me to enter into any familiarity with them. I have loved individuals, I have never much cared for men in the mass. I have none of that engaging come-hitherness that makes people take to one another on first acquaintance. Though in the course of years I have learnt to assume an air of heartiness when forced into contact with a stranger, I have never liked anyone at first sight. I do not think I have never [*sic*] addressed some one I did not know in a rail-way carriage or spoken to a fellow passenger on board ship unless he first spoke to me. The weakness of my flesh has prevented me from enjoying that communion with the human race that is engendered by alcohol.[17]

Again:

My sympathies are limited. I can only be myself, and partly by nature, partly by the circumstances of my life, it is a partial self. I am not a social person . . . convivial amusement has always somewhat bored me. When people sit in an ale house or drifting down the river in a boat start singing I am silent. I have never even sung a hymn. I do not much like being touched and I have always to make a slight effort over myself not to draw away when someone links his arm in mine. I can never forget myself. The hysteria of the world repels me and I never feel more aloof than when I am in the midst of a throng surrendered to a violent feeling of mirth or sorrow. Though I have been in love a good many times, I have never experienced the bliss of requited love . . . I have most loved people who cared little or nothing for me and when people have loved me, I have been embarassed. It has been a predicament that I have not quite known how to deal with . . . I have tried, with gentleness when possible, and if not, with irritation, to escape from the trammels with which their love bound me. I have been jealous of my independence. I am incapable of complete surrender.[18]

17 *Ibid.*, 32.
18 *Ibid.*, 53.

What influences have gone into the make-up of such a personality as this? First, the influence of Maugham's unhappy childhood and adolescence: The early death of his parents seems to have created a void in his emotional life which was probably never adequately replenished. Starved of affection in the most impressionable years of his life, Maugham presented the tragic spectacle of a man who had lost the capacity to love deeply and truly. This was also indicated by his general attitude towards love which emerges from a survey of his work—a topic which will be discussed in chapter X.

The sense of loneliness which shaped Maugham's attitude toward men and the world and which frequently found expression in cynical indifference also seems to have originated in his orphaned childhood and adolescence. The physical disability from which the boy suffered was at once the cause and the result of this early unhappiness. If stammering, as psychologists tell us, is not a disability due to organic conditions, but a neurotic disturbance that usually occurs at an early age in a high-strung individual, the relationship between Maugham's unhappy childhood and adolescence and his stammer becomes quite discernible.

In *Ten Novels and Their Authors*, where Maugham examines the work of some of the greatest novelists of the world, he considers the question as to how far a physical disability can affect an author's work.

> I have no doubt that a physical or spiritual disability affects the character of an author's work. To some extent it sets him apart from his fellows, makes him self-conscious, prejudices him, so that he sees the world, life and his fellow-creatures from a standpoint, often unduly jejune, which is not the usual one. . . . I do not doubt that Dostoevsky would not have written the sort of books he did if he had not been an epileptic.[19]

[19] Page 299.

These remarks have a curious pertinence to Maugham's own personality and work.

Even more pertinent is Maugham's explicit confession in *A Writer's Notebook*:

> I think many people shrink from the notion that the accidents of the body can have an effect on the constitution of the soul. There is nothing of which for my own part I am more assured. My soul would have been quite different if I had not stammered or if I had been four or five inches taller. I am slightly prognathous; in my childhood they did not know that this could be remedied by a gold band worn while the jaw is still malleable; if they had, my countenance would have borne a different cast, the reaction towards me of my fellows would have been different too.[20]

Philip Carey's clubfoot and the account of how the disability made him a shy, self-conscious, and self-centered adolescent have a close parallel in his creator's own adolescence. Thus, the aloofness and reserve, the tendency to be on his guard against passion and sympathy, and the cold indifference which appear to characterize most of Maugham's work could be explained, in a measure, in terms of this early unhappiness and the factors which contributed to it.

Another significant influence on Maugham was his travels. He was probably one of the most widely traveled authors among modern English writers. He had journeyed to several parts of the world and had visited each for long periods—China, Malaya, the South Sea Islands, Burma, India, Spain, Russia, and the United States. "I travelled," says Maugham, "because it amused me, and to get material that would be of use to me."[21] "I have had small power of imagination," he confesses in his candid

[20] Page 293.
[21] *The Summing Up*, 140.

way, and "I have taken living people and put them into the situations tragic or comic that their characters suggested."[22]

It was to collect these living specimens that Maugham traveled. He certainly made a priceless collection, and the variety of scene and setting and of character and culture is one of the main charms of his work. Novels like *The Narrow Corner, The Moon and Sixpence, The Painted Veil,* and *Up at the Villa,* plays like *East of Suez* and *Caesar's Wife,* and short stories like "Red," "Rain," "The Pool," and "Mr. Harrington's Washing" exploit skilfully the charm of a distant setting, whether in Malaya, the South Sea Islands, China, or Russia.

Travel also furnished Maugham with certain types of characters which appear again and again in his books: the British civilian in the East; the European conquered by the beauty and mystery of the Orient, or destroyed in the attempt to adjust to its ways; the beachcomber who is by temperament and necessity a rogue and a scoundrel; and the missionary, earnest but misguided, or shifty and worldly.

But of more significance is this statement by Maugham:

> . . . my new experiences were having an effect on me, and it was not till long afterwards that I saw how they had formed my character. In contact with all these strange people I lost the smoothness that I had acquired when, leading the humdrum life of a man of letters, I was one of the stones in a bag. I got back my jagged edges. I was at last myself. I ceased to travel because I felt that travel could give me nothing more. I was capable of no new development. I had sloughed the arrogance of culture. My mood was complete acceptance. I asked from nobody more than he could give me. I had learnt toleration. I was pleased with the goodness of my fellows; I was not distressed by their badness. I had acquired independence of spirit. I had to go my way without bothering with what others thought

[22] *Ibid.,* 56.

about it. I demanded freedom for myself and I was prepared to give freedom to others.[23]

It is not difficult to realize how the frigid indifference and aloofness of Maugham was the product of his travels, for between the "toleration" and "complete acceptance," which Maugham said travel had taught him, and cynical indifference lies but a thin dividing line.

It is also possible to interpret Maugham's passion for travel in the light of his loneliness and lack of roots consequent on the breakup of his home during childhood.

> I am attached to England, but I have never felt myself very much at home there. I have always been shy with English people. To me England has been a country where I had obligations that I did not want to fulfil and responsibilities that irked me. Some fortunate persons find freedom in their own minds; I, with less spiritual power than they find it in travel.[24]

What Maugham thought to be freedom may also have been an effort to forget his sense of loneliness and of lack of roots in life. Travel thus shaped Maugham's general attitude toward men and the world to a considerable extent.

The French influence played an equally important role in molding the artistic make-up of Maugham. In several ways he appeared to be more French than English, and it is significant to note that when he thought of settling down permanently, he chose France as his home. As noted earlier, born in Paris, he spent his early childhood in France, spoke French before he spoke English, and attended a French school. "It was France that educated me," he declared, "France that taught me to value beauty, distinction, wit and good sense, France that taught

23 *Ibid.*, 140–41.
24 *Ibid.*, 66.

me to write."[25] And again, "I studied the French novelists more than the English."[26]

Among the French novelists, he makes special mention of Maupassant: "It was the novels and short stories of Guy de Maupassant that had most influence on me when I set myself to write. I began to read them when I was sixteen."[27] He goes on to say how, whenever he went to Paris, he spent his afternoons in the galleries of the Odeon, purchasing the cheaper of Maupassant's books and hurrying through the more costly ones, while standing before the shelves. He had thus managed to read most of Maupassant before he was twenty. Desmond Mac-Carthy calls Maugham "The English Maupassant," and the parallel is very apt, for Maupassant's unflinching realism, the wealth of human character which his work shows, his lucidity and sense of construction, and even the charge of cynicism leveled against his work—all these, more or less, are also the characteristics of the work of the "English Maupassant."

In a review of *A Writer's Notebook*, V. S. Pritchett makes the illuminating suggestion that in Mérimée "lies his [Maugham's] real master, and a character astonishingly like his own."[28] Maugham and Mérimée indeed appear to be kindred spirits in more than one way. First, just as Maugham is an Englishman with a strong French strain in his mental make-up, so was Mérimée a Frenchman with a strain of English blood, and English phlegm, in him. Further, like Maugham's mind, Mérimée's was capable of strong sensibility and yet strangely afraid of passion and excess. This sensibility, so clearly seen in Mérimée's letters to an "unknown lady" (now known to have been Mlle Jenny Dacquin), was severely suppressed, leading Mérimée to cultivate a studiedly impartial objectivity, very

[25] Quoted by John Brophy, *Somerset Maugham*, 8.
[26] *The Summing Up*, 115.
[27] *Ibid.*, 115.
[28] *The Author*, Vol. LX, No. 3, p. 75.

often resulting, as in Maugham's case, in indifference and coldness. Again, as in Maugham, Mérimée's detachment was an ironical detachment, and his irony, like Maugham's, was both sharp and polished. Lastly, Mérimée, too, was a born storyteller, with a terse, witty, and clear style.

Whether it was Maupassant or Mérimée who was Maugham's real master, the fact remains that Maugham's work as a whole has greater affinity with the ethos of French rather than of English literature. In his general outlook on the world, in his valuing and asserting reason over emotion, in his methods of studying and presenting human character, in his keen sense of irony, in his preoccupation with perfection of form, and in the clarity and precision of his style, Maugham seems to be more French than English. It is highly significant that France has admired, appreciated, and honored Maugham to a greater extent than England—He was a commander of the French Legion of Honour.

Such, then, is the picture of Maugham's life and of the influences which seem to have shaped his personality. Strains which may possibly have led to cynicism are apparent. Early frustration and suffering often lead to cynicism; and cynicism, from the psychological point of view, is sometimes the defense reaction of a sensitive mind against its own sensitivity. It is possible to see both of these in Maugham's personality, as also the resulting "disposition to look upon human life and morals with frigid indifference," and the lack of warmth, which have been already noted among the distinguishing marks of cynicism.

CHAPTER THREE

Early Novels and Plays

·

THE EARLY NOVELS and plays of Maugham show the twin strains of cynicism and humanitarianism at work. Of the early novels, eight in all,[1] Maugham, until his last years, believed only two worth including in the collected edition of his works, and rightly so, for of these early novels only *Liza of Lambeth* and *Mrs. Craddock* were successful, and they do indeed attain a level of achievement which the other six novels, for one reason or another, fail to reach.[2] Two of these novels can be dismissed at once: The first, *The Bishop's Apron*, was a novelization of the play *Loaves and Fishes*, written in 1902 and rejected by managers until it was staged in 1911; the second, *The Explorer*, was based upon a play of the same name, written in 1907. About these novelizations Maugham candidly says that "for long they lay on my conscience like a discreditable action. I would have given much to suppress them."[3]

The fate of the other four unsuccessful novels is also soon told. In *The Making of a Saint*, Maugham sought to write a

[1] Novels: *Liza of Lambeth* (1897); *The Making of a Saint* (1898); *The Hero* (1901); *Mrs. Craddock* (1902); *The Merry-Go-Round* (1904); *The Bishop's Apron* (1906); *The Explorer* (1908); *The Magician* (1908).

Plays: *Loaves and Fishes* (written 1902, published 1924); *A Man of Honour* (1903); *Lady Frederick* (1912); *Jack Straw* (1912); *Mrs. Dot* (1912); *Penelope* (1912); *The Explorer* (1912); *The Tenth Man* (1913); *Landed Gentry* (1913); *Smith* (1913); *The Land of Promise* (1913).

[2] In 1956, Maugham decided to include *The Magician* in the collected edition of his works.

[3] *The Summing Up*, 114.

historical romance set against the background of the Italian Renaissance. He did so because, as he tells us in *The Summing Up*, he thought at the time that "the historical novel was the only one that the young author could hope to write with success, for he could not have sufficient experience of life to write of contemporary manners"[4]—an extremely curious explanation. The novel fails simply because a romance of adventure and hairbreadth escapes was not, and never could have been, Maugham's province.

The Hero has Kent for its setting, but even though Kent is the scene of Maugham's childhood, the book is marred by lifeless characters. The Kent setting was to be used to far greater advantage in *Mrs. Craddock* and *Of Human Bondage*. The failure of *The Merry-Go-Round* is due to an unsuccessful technical experiment. Several plots are connected together by a very thin thread, viz., a character who knows at least one person in each group. The result is the diffusion of interest among many characters and actions. To make matters worse, the book was written, as Maugham himself confessed, "in a tight and affected manner"[5] after the preciosity of the Aesthetic School of the 1890's.

The Magician, the last of the unsuccessful novels, purports to be an exercise in the occult. The character of the wizard was based upon that of Aleister Crowley, whose life was written by John Symonds under the title *The Great Beast* (1951). In a preface written upon the inclusion of the novel in the collected edition of his works, Maugham wrote that when he had reread it after fifty years, "it held my interest, as two of my early novels, which, for the same reason I have been obliged to read, did not."[6] We are also told how, as he read it, "I wondered how on

4 *Ibid.*, 112.
5 *Ibid.*, 116.
6 *A Fragment of Autobiography*, ix.

earth I could have come by all the material concerning the black arts which I wrote of."[7] Nevertheless, *The Magician* is vitiated at the core by the author's ambivalent attitude to his subject. In the novel, Arthur says to Dr. Porhoët, "I never know how much you really believe of all these things you tell us. You speak with such gravity that we are all taken in, and then it turns out that you've been laughing at us."[8] This is precisely the reader's complaint against Maugham in *The Magician*. The Gothic novel was not exactly Maugham's forte, and he was wise not to repeat the experiment.

In the two successful novels, *Liza of Lambeth* and *Mrs. Craddock*, there is a rich strain of compassion. Their settings differ: Liza is a child of the Lambeth slums and low-class factory life, while Bertha Craddock is the daughter of a country squire in a quiet provincial town on the sea coast of Kent. But both are women who love passionately and suffer, and the picture of their suffering is drawn with deep understanding and sympathy.

From the point of view of artistic technique, *Liza of Lambeth* is crude and immature. Maugham himself made very modest claims for it.

> Any merit it may have is due to the luck I had in being, by my work as a medical student, thrown into contact with a side of life that at that time had been little exploited by novelists. Arthur Morrison, with his *Tales of Mean Street* and *A Child of the Jago* had drawn the attention of the public to what were then known as the lower classes, and I profited by the interest he had aroused.[9]

In places, *Liza of Lambeth* indeed reads less like a novel than a transcript from slum life. Its strength, however, lies in the por-

[7] *Ibid.*, x.
[8] *The Magician*, 54.
[9] *The Summing Up*, 111.

trait of Liza and in the picture of slum life, both of which are done with restraint and realism, and yet with understanding and compassion.

When Liza first appears on the scene, she is just a youthful, energetic, good-natured, and cheerful girl of eighteen, with a fair share of feminine vanity which she shows in swaggering through the street in her new dress on Saturday afternoon, proud of the sensation she is creating.

> Every one liked her and was glad to have her company. "Good old Liza," they would say, as she left them, "she is a rare good sort, ain't she?" She asked after the aches and pains of all the old people and delicately inquired after the babies, past and future; the children hung on to her skirts and asked her to play with them, and she would hold one end of the rope while tiny little girls skipped, invariably entangling themselves after two jumps.[10]

She rejects Tom, who loves her, but notices that she has pained him. "She could not see the look upon his face, but she heard the agony in his voice; and moved with sudden pity, she bent out, threw her arms around his neck, and kissed him on both cheeks." "Never mind, old chap!" she said, "I am not worth troublin' abaht."[11] But for all this, Liza is by no means an angel of goodness and innocence. She is a shrewd and practical young girl: she realizes that if she tells her mother where she hid her week's pay, it will get " 'perspired like' [i.e., evaporated] [and] she cooly tells Mrs. Kemp next time that the money has been put away 'where it will be safe.' "

This young woman, with her abundant zest for life, requires a strong man full of animal vitality to rouse the springs of love within her. Tom, however, who is shy and unassuming, is dismissed by Liza with the words, "I don't want him slob-

10 *Liza of Lambeth,* 28.
11 *Ibid.,* 19.

berin' abaht me; it gives me the sick, all this kissin' and cuddlin'!"[12] Love enters into Liza's life with Jim Blakeston, tall, broad-shouldered, and bearded, and she surrenders herself wholeheartedly to her whirlwind passion for a man who is forty and the father of one-half dozen children. "I couldn't help it," she confesses to Tom, "I did love 'im so."[13] The inevitable happens, Liza becomes pregnant and dies from the effects of an abortion. Maugham makes no attempt to whitewash Liza, nor is there any Hardean cry of "a pure woman" over the fallen girl. Her death is described in a quiet, restrained way, and no tears are shed over this "one more unfortunate." Yet, the author's deep sympathy for the Lambeth girl saves the picture from becoming sordid in the worst Zolaesque manner.

The portrayal of slum life in the novel is also done in the same spirit. It is a thoroughly realistic picture, without any glossing over or sentimentalizing. Maughan avoids the pitfall of looking only at sordidness and revelling in it—a weakness of a certain type of realism. Both the humor and the pathos of slum life are shown. Liza's mother, a martyr to "rheumatics," and Mrs. Hodges, the midwife, with whom she discusses the advantages of insuring one's children and the relative merits of oak and elm coffins, while Liza is on her deathbed, represent the rough humor of the slums.

Misery is the "daily food" of the people of Lambeth. (Maugham tells us in the preface to a new edition of *Liza* [1951] that the Lambeth of 1897 has now vanished.) There marriage means six days of sobriety followed by drunkenness, and Saturday night is "the time when women in the Vere street weep."[14] There "'usbinds [husbands] is all alike; they're arright when they're sober—sometimes—but when they've got the

12 *Ibid.*, 49.
13 *Ibid.*, 138.
14 *Ibid.*, 119–20.

liquor in 'em, they're beasts, an' no mistake."[15] The philosophy of wife-beating, as seen through the eyes of a wife, is: "I can stand a blow as well as any woman. I don't mind that, an' when 'e don't tike [take] a mean advantage of me I can stand up for myself an' give as good as I like."[16]

The coming of babies is the commonest topic of conversation in Lambeth, for a wife is always either nursing a baby or expecting one, and often doing both. Apart from the humor and the pathos of slum life, the sports and pleasures of the people are likewise described with gusto and understanding. The outing on bank holiday, where one of the sports is a contest in spitting; the dancing at the street corner when the Italian organ-grinder arrives; the delights of the penny melodrama at the theater; the street fights; and the improvised cricket matches in the lanes with coats as stumps—all these are described clearly and vividly.

Bertha, the heroine of *Mrs. Craddock* is also a victim of love, but her mind differs substantially from that of the simple Liza. She is a sophisticated young woman whose childhood was spent in wandering about the Continent, and she was "educated in half a dozen countries." In her peculiar upbringing, she never experienced the restraints which normally shape the personality of the daughter of a country squire. She became an independent and self-willed young woman.

The birth of love in Bertha's heart has a strange effect on her. It becomes a consuming hunger and thirst—a hunger to surrender herself, body and soul, to a strong male. Bertha thinks that she has found her mate in the massive and big-boned gentleman-farmer Edward Craddock. She inhales voluptuously "the pleasant odour of the farmyard, the mingled perfume of strong tobacco, of cattle and horses" which he always brings

---

[15] *Ibid.,* 121.
[16] *Ibid.,* 71.

with him. Bertha brooks no opposition to her desire to marry Edward; she ignores murmurs of *"mésalliance,"* and declares to her guardians, "I care nothing for his reputation. If he were drunken and idle and dissolute, I'd marry him because I love him."[17]

Indeed, so in love was Bertha with Edward that she "wanted to abase herself before the strong man, to be low and humble before him. She would have been his handmaiden, and nothing could have satisfied her so much as to perform for him menial services. She knew not how to show the immensity of her passion."[18] Hence, "Bertha gave herself over completely to the enjoyment of her love. . . . love was a great sea into which she boldly plunged, uncaring whether she would swim or sink."[19] "He was the man and she was the woman, and the world was a garden of Eden conjured up by the power of passion."[20] "My love will never alter," she is sure, "It is too strong. To the end of my days I shall always love you with all my heart."[21]

Edward's limitations are transmuted into virtues in Bertha's powerful imagination—his ignorance and naïveté into simplicity and innocence, and his vulgarity of taste into freedom from sophistication. The first few months of married life are "an exquisite dream" for Bertha.

Then suddenly comes the rude awakening. Bertha realizes that a yawning gulf separates her passionate self from her cold and prosaic husband. "Love to her was a fire, a flame that absorbed the rest of life; love to him was a convenient and necessary institution of Providence, a matter about which there was as little need of excitement as about the ordering of a new suit

[17] *Mrs. Craddock*, 24.
[18] *Ibid.*, 38–45.
[19] *Ibid.*, 46.
[20] *Ibid.*, 83.
[21] *Ibid.*, 55.

of clothes."[22] As Miss Ley, Bertha's maiden aunt, says, "For Bertha the book of life is written throughout in italics; for Edward it is all in the big round hand of the copy-book heading."[23]

Now begin Bertha's tribulations. She tries to inspire Edward with her own fire, but fails and feels humiliated. Then a cold fear seizes her: Edward neither loved nor had ever loved her. "She told herself that she could not do things by halves, she must love or detest, but in either case, fiercely." She now "wavered uncertainly between the old passionate devotion and a new equally passionate hatred."[24]

Bertha's knowledge that she is with child brings new hope of securing a worthier object on which she can bestow her affection, but the child is still-born, and, what is worse, Bertha is told that she can never have another child. She once more turns to Edward, transferring to him "the tenderness that she had lavished on her dead child, and all the yearning that must now, to her life's end, go unsatisfied."[25] Once more she is disappointed, but this time the disappointment is as great as her new yearning has been fierce. Under the blow, "suddenly she abhorred him; the love that had been a tower of brass, fell like a house of cards. . . . Bertha found a bitter fascination in stripping her idol of the finery with which her madness had bedizened him."[26]

Hate and love are twins, however, and in the extreme physical and mental exhaustion which follows her delivery, Bertha's moods alternate between the two. Thus, she decides to leave her husband for good and journeys to London, but, after a stay of six weeks, comes back, because in the struggle in her heart,

22 *Ibid.*, 199.
23 *Ibid.*, 106.
24 *Ibid.*, 120.
25 *Ibid.*, 157.
26 *Ibid.*, 163.

35

"Pride, anger, reason, everything had been on one side and only love on the other; and love had conquered."[27] But the six-week-long separation gives Bertha a new perspective. When she meets Edward again, she does not see the slender, manly youth whom she had loved; instead, she sees before her a heavy and coarse country farmer. The seesaw of hate and love ends, and "Bertha's love, indeed, had finally disappeared as suddenly as it had arisen, and she began to detest her husband."[28] Each of Edward's faults now becomes magnified in her eyes, and she wonders how she ever loved this man and humbled herself so abjectly before such a creature. To be free from love of him and indifferent is a great satisfaction.

Mrs. Craddock, however, is a woman made for intense love. She soon finds another object which, she feels, is worthier to receive this love. She meets her young scamp of a cousin— Gerald—in London, where she has once more fled from Edward and the country. Gerald, nineteen and happy-go-lucky, flirts with her, little knowing that he is playing with fire. The fires of passion, rekindled in Bertha, are about to consume both her and Gerald, but the watchfulness of her aunt and Gerald's inexperience save them.

Disappointed again and broken in spirit, Bertha returns to the monotony of country life. A murky pall of ennui settles on her soul, and, like Hardy's Viviette in *Two on a Tower*, placed against a similar background, she is "a walking weariness." Nothing can dispel it, not even the sudden death of Edward in an accident.

Bertha's passionate nature threatens to bring on her a curious revenge when, left alone, she turns back to the past— to the Edward of the first few days of their association. She now begins to fear that all her love for him will return and gnaw at

[27] *Ibid.*, 194.
[28] *Ibid.*, 198.

her heart forever. In a wild frenzy, she seeks to shatter the past
and begin a new life. She burns all his letters and photographs,
gives up their home, and becomes a wanderer. Her struggles
are now over, the fires in her heart are burned out. She is ex-
hausted and world-weary. "Her apathetic eyes said that she had
loved and found love wanting, that she had been a mother and
that her child had died, and that now she desired nothing very
much but to be left in peace."[29]

The analysis of Bertha's changing moods is done with
great subtlety, but what is more significant is the fact that
Bertha herself, though abnormal, never loses our sympathy
even when we realize that the demands she makes on her
pedestrian-but-honest husband are excessive.

In Liza and Bertha, Maugham painted two women con-
sumed by passion. In Kitty (*The Painted Veil*, 1925) and
Julia (*The Theatre*, 1937), he was to return virtually to the
same theme. But, in the meantime, cynicism had won, and to
sympathize with Kitty and Julia is as impossible as not to
sympathize with Liza and Bertha.

Another significant aspect of *Mrs. Craddock* is that it also
shows the other strain in Maugham—the cynical strain, or
something akin to it. It is in the portraiture of Miss Ley, Bertha's
maiden aunt that this other self of Maugham is first fully revealed. In fact, Miss Ley is an early indication of the cynical
propensities in Maugham.[30]

Miss Ley is a middle-aged, well-to-do spinster, with thin
lips and a tightly compressed mouth. "She had a habit of fixing
her cold eyes on people with a steadiness that was not a little
embarassing. They said Miss Ley looked as if she thought them
great fools and as a matter of fact that usually was precisely

[29] *Ibid.*, 300.
[30] Susie Boyd in *The Magician* begins as a spiritual sister to Miss Ley, but
becomes a conventional lover by the end of the novel.

what she did think."[31] She has a disconcerting habit of "saying
rather absurd things in the gravest and most decorous manner."
Human beings interest her because, as she puts it, "they are so
stupid." But though she is interested in human nature, she also
believes that "one's greatest duty in this world is to leave people
alone." She wishes nothing more than "to leave people alone
and be left alone by them." Miss Ley is a sentimentalist at war
with her own sentimentalism.

> Like the Red Indian who will suffer the most horrid tortures
> without wincing, Miss Ley would have thought it highly dis-
> graceful to display feeling at some touching scene. She used
> polite cynicism as a cloak for sentimentality, laughing that she
> might not cry . . . she felt that tears were unbecoming and
> foolish.[32]

Love and marriage are summed up for Miss Ley in two
phrases, "the instinct of reproduction" and "the female attracted to the male." Her whole attitude towards life is "a
shrug of shoulders and a well-bred smile of contempt." Her
idea of a happy life is "to gather the roses—with gloves on, so
that the thorns should not prick me." It is significant that Miss
Ley quotes Rochefoucauld, and that her favorite author is
Montaigne.

There is much that can be said for Miss Ley's philosophy of
life. It helps her eminently in preserving her liberty and in
dealing with people in general. But it is in Miss Ley's relations
with Bertha that the limitations of her attitude toward life are
exposed. Bertha's struggles interest her, but she can hardly
comprehend their true significance. Even when she saves Bertha
from getting into mischief with Gerald, her motive in doing so
is not so much love for her niece as the desire to avoid the

[31] *Mrs. Craddock,* 9–10.
[32] *Ibid.,* 2–3.

complications which might upset the even tenor of her own life.

The limitations of her philosophy of life are not fully revealed until she appears for the last time in the novel. When Bertha, weary and disappointed, sets out for home again, the only thing that Miss Ley has to offer her is a string of polite platitudes about the desirability of treading the safest path in life;[33] and her conclusion of the whole matter is—"The fact is that very few women can be happy with only one husband. I believe that the only solution of the marriage question is legalised polyandry"—a diverting thought indeed; but it also shows how the sentimentalist turning savagely against himself manages to murder all sympathy in his breast and become a cold, indifferent cynic.

From among the eleven plays of the first phase of his career as a dramatist, Maugham included only six in the collected edition of his works. They are: *Lady Frederick, Jack Straw, Mrs. Dot,* and *Penelope* (1912), and *Smith* and *The Land of Promise* (1913). The themes of the first three, of which *Jack Straw* and *Mrs. Dot* are both described as "farces" by their author, are amusing but trivial, each with a touch of light satire and sentiment.

Lady Frederick portrays "an adventuress with a heart of gold"; *Mrs. Dot* is a sketch of an intelligent woman who employs a variety of tricks to catch her man; *Jack Straw* is built round the hoary comic convention of mistaken identity. They are plays after the manner of Oscar Wilde, but of the Wilde of the early comedies, not of the Wilde of *The Importance of Being Earnest*. They have more of lighthearted flippancy than of satire or cynicism. The portrayal of upper-class society in these plays has nothing of the bitterness and savagery of the later plays. Even the so-called confirmed cynics in these plays—

[33] *Ibid.,* 268–69.

Paradine Fouldes in *Mrs. Frederick* and Blenkinsop in *Mrs. Dot*—are harmless middle-aged bachelors indulging (like Lord Goring in *An Ideal Husband*,) in nothing stronger than a few flippant and innocuous epigrams and paradoxes.

The lack of depth in these early plays is even better illustrated by *Jack Straw*. Here, in exposing the snobs—Mr. and Mrs. Parker-Jennings—the author is as kind to them as he is cruel to the snobs in his later plays. The Parker-Jennings are vulgar and mean-minded upstarts in whom a windfall prompts a passion for hobnobbing with the aristocracy. A hotel waiter is passed off on them as an archduke. But their discomfiture is not severe. Being consistently compatible with the geniality of the play, the supposed waiter turns out to be the Archduke of Pomeranid. Satire thus melts into good spirits. Each of the three plays ends with a marriage, providing a fine contrast with the endings of some of the bitter comedies of Maugham's second phase. About these three plays Maugham wrote:

> I had then very high spirits, a facility for amusing dialogue, an eye for a comic situation, and a flippant gaiety; there was more in me than that, but this I put away for the time and wrote my comedies with those sides of myself only that were useful to my purpose. They were designed to please and they achieved their aim.[34]

Maugham's progress from *Lady Frederick* to *Penelope* had an almost exact parallel in Oscar Wilde's advance from light sentimental comedy in *Lady Windermere's Fan* to an intellectual comedy of manners in *The Importance of Being Earnest*. *Lady Frederick* and its two immediate successors have their share of sentiment, and rather cheap sentiment it is. Peculiar things happen in the world of these comedies. Here, a debt-ridden siren is magnanimous enough to let her prey escape

[34] *The Summing Up,* 81.

(Lady Frederick); a confirmed cynic suddenly becomes an ardent lover (Paradine Fouldes); an archduke (Jack Straw) falls in love with and marries the daughter of an upstart because she is kind to him when he, disguised as a waiter, is shamefully treated by her parents.

In *Penelope*, Maugham rose above sham sentiment, though he is still far from being bitter and cruel, as in some of the later comedies. The title of the play is significant. Penelope is the devoted wife, the Penelope of the *Odyssey*. The problem of the play, stated in rather simple terms, is, "How can a wife keep her husband's love?" The answer given by Professor Golightly in the play is that "a wise woman never lets her husband be quite, quite sure of her. The moment he is, Cupid puts on a top-hat and becomes a church-warden." His advice to Penelope is not to make her love too cheap: "Remember that man is by nature a hunter. But how can he pursue if you're always flinging yourself in his arm? . . . Make yourself a fortress that must be freshly stormed each day."[35] But the problem is throughout dealt with on the purely intellectual plane, in the best tradition of the comedy of manners. *Penelope* has, therefore, neither sentiment nor satire. It is Maugham's *The Importance of Being Earnest*.

The theme in both *Smith* and *The Land of Promise* is almost identical—the contrast between the artificial, hothouse life and false values of upper middle-class society and the healthy, natural life and true values of the farmers in the colonies who struggle with Nature to turn a wilderness into cultivated land. But the theme is treated differently in each play. There is no satire in *The Land of Promise*, which tells in a straightforward manner the story of Norah Marsh, who is compelled by circumstances to give up the idle and dull but secure and comfortable life of a lady's companion in England

[35] *Penelope, Collected plays*, Vol. II, 82.

for the hard and rough but useful life of a farmer's wife in
Canada. It is not easy for her to accustom herself to her new
way of life. Yet, when that is done, she begins to love her new
life so well that she forgoes an opportunity to return to her old
life and remarks:

> I know the life now. It's not adventurous and exciting. For
> men and women it is the same hard work from morning till
> night, and I know it's the women who bear the greater burden.
> . . . And yet it's all got a meaning. We, too, have our part in
> opening up the country. We are its mothers and the future is
> in us. We are building up the greatness of the nation. It needs
> our courage and strength and hope, and because it needs them,
> they come to us.[36]

The purpose of *Smith* is to expose the false values of upper
middle-class life by viewing them through the eyes of a young
Rhodesian farmer, Thomas Freeman, who has returned to
England in search of a wife. He finds himself in a thoroughly
decadent society, where a lady does not want to have a child
because "it would bore me to death," where a mother would
rather attend a bridge party than stay with her sick child, where
the day is considered to be well spent in paying idle calls and
visiting the dressmaker, where the only objective of conversation is tearing the reputation of absent friends to pieces, where
work is considered to be "merely the refuge from boredom of
the unintellectual," and where young men delight in becoming
social parasites and hangers-on of married couples, who are
satisfied with the arrangement, because to have a young man
with whom to flirt makes for some occupation for the wife and
peace to the husband. At the conclusion of the play Thomas
Freeman says:

> It took me some time to discover that you weren't real people
> at all. You're not men and women but strange sexless creatures,

[36] *The Land of Promise, Collected Plays,* Vol. I, 308.

without blood in your veins. . . . You're too trifling to be wicked.
. . . In yourself you're perfectly unimportant, but England is
full of people as flippant and frivolous and inane as yourself.[37]

The note of satire is stronger here than in any of the preceding comedies, but the positive values are indicated through
Thomas Freeman. This is not done—at least not done with
equal power, as will be shown later on—in some of the later
comedies, which therefore lie open to the charge of cynicism.

Of the five plays not included in the collected edition,
three may be briefly noticed. *Loaves and Fishes,* written as early
as 1902, though published much later (1924), is a minor play,
a light farcical satire on the clergy—Maugham's favorite butt.
Of the other two, *The Tenth Man* and *Landed Gentry,*
Maugham says:

> . . . [they] fell between two stools. One portrayed the narrow,
> hide-bound life of country gentlefolk; the other, the political
> and financial world; with both of which I had some acquaint-
> ance. I knew that I must interest, move and amuse, and I
> heightened the note. They were neither frankly realistic nor
> frankly theatrical. My indecision was fatal. The audiences
> found them rather disagreeable and not quite real.[38]

The first phase of Maugham's work—his early novels and
plays—may now be summed up in the light of the conflict between cynicism and humanitarianism. Maugham's native sensibility appears to be very strong during this phase for it portrays
both Liza of Lambeth and Mrs. Craddock with deep compassion and tenderness. But since reticence, reserve, and restraint are innate in Maugham, he avoids the pitfall of sentimentalism in both the novels. There is, as has been shown,
some cheap sentiment in several of the early comedies (*Lady
Frederick, Jack Straw,* and *Mrs. Dot*), but it is, as Maugham

[37] *Smith, Collected Plays,* Vol. I, 202.
[38] *The Summing Up,* 82.

himself remarked, the result of a deliberate attempt on his part to give to the public what it wanted.[39]

The other strain which, later on, was to develop, at least in some places, into cynicism, also makes its appearance in this phase. It is present, first of all, in the portrayal of Miss Ley in *Mrs. Craddock*, in whom Maugham seemed to have put much of his other self. Miss Ley, the sentimentalist-turned-cynic, looking at Bertha's tribulations with her frigid indifference and her sneers, seems to be a projection of Maugham's cynical self looking at the sympathetic picture painted by his native sensibility. The author's sensibility wins this phase of the conflict, for though the character of Miss Ley interests us, it is Bertha who runs away with our hearts.

The cynical strain also appears in some of the unsuccessful novels of the early period—as in the cynical observations on the mob in *The Making of a Saint*, in the crude iconoclasm of James Parsons in *The Hero*, and in the attack on the clergy in *The Bishop's Apron*. But since these novels fail to come to life, their cynicism, too, fails to be effective and only appears to be the efforts of a clever young man's desire to shock.

In the early plays, sheer gaiety and harmless flippancy predominate in the lighter pieces such as *Lady Frederick*. In *Penelope*, Maugham achieved pure comedy which rises above both sentiment and satire. *The Land of Promise*, wholly serious in tone, has no room for either humor or satire. It is only in *Smith* that satire dominates. Here is powerful satire, but no cynicism, because the positive values are kept in sight throughout.

The work of this early phase does not show any great positive achievement, but it does reveal considerable promise. Maugham the artist was still learning his trade. Hence, it is the straightforward, undistinguished method of narration in both

[39] *Ibid.*, 81.

Liza of Lambeth and *Mrs. Craddock* that appears to be crude, especially if compared with the dexterously woven and intricate patterns in, say, *Cakes and Ale*. Yet, this early work illustrates the two faculties in Maugham—the deep sensibility which was, very soon, to create a book which ranks among the best of Maugham's novels, *Of Human Bondage,* and the flair for satirical observation which was to find full scope in the sardonic comedies of the later years and develop into the cold indifference and cynicism of some of his later works.

CHAPTER FOUR

Of Human Bondage

.

T HE STRONG NATIVE SENSIBILITY which dominates the works of Maugham's early phase reaches its high-water mark in *Of Human Bondage*,[1] a novel which is largely autobiographical. Maugham wrote in *The Summing Up* that, having finished the novel, he "prepared to make a fresh start."[2] This "fresh start" was to lead him far away from the dominant strain in *Liza of Lambeth, Mrs. Craddock,* and *Of Human Bondage*.

Maugham described the genesis of this novel in *The Summing Up* and also in the introduction to the reprint of the novel in the Collected Edition of his works. We are told that Maugham first wrote *Of Human Bondage* in a much shorter form, as early as 1897–98:

> It was called then, somewhat grandly, "The Artistic Temperament of Stephen Carey." It finished with the hero at the age of twenty-four, which was my own age when I finished it, and it sent him to Rouen, which I knew only from two or three short visits to see the sights, instead of Heidelberg, as in *Of Human Bondage*, which I knew well; and it made him study music, of which I knew nothing, instead of making him study painting, of which in later years I was to learn at least a little.[3]

The book was rejected by publishers and was put aside. But, continues Maugham:

[1] 1915. [2] Page 131.
[3] *Of Human Bondage*, "Collected Edition," v.

I could not forget the people, the incidents and the emotions of which it was composed. In the next ten years I had other experiences and met other people. The book continued to write itself in my mind, and many things that happened to me found their place in it. Certain of my recollections were so insistent that, waking or sleeping, I could not escape from them. I was by then a popular playwright. I was making for those days a great deal of money, and the managers could hardly wait to engage a cast till I had written the last act of my new piece. But my memories would not let me be. They became such a torment that I determined at last to have done with the theatre till I had released myself from them. My book took me two years to write. I was disconcerted at the unwieldly length to which it seemed to be extending, but I was not writing to please; I was writing to free myself of an intolerable obsession. I achieved the result I aimed at, for after I had corrected the proofs, I found all those ghosts were laid, and neither the people who played their parts in the story, nor the incidents in which they were concerned ever crossed my mind again. Looking back on it now in memory[4] . . . I can hardly tell what is fancy and what is fact, what parts describe events that happened, sometimes accurately and sometimes disturbed by an anxious imagination, and what parts describe what I could have wished had happened.[5]

The account in *The Summing Up* is even more explicit. Maugham narrates there how, at the height of his success as a playwright, he began to be obsessed by:

. . . the teeming memories of my past life. The loss of my mother and then the break up of my home, the wretchedness of my first years at the school for which my French childhood had so ill-prepared me, and which my stammering made so difficult, the delight of those easy, monotonous and exciting days in Heidelberg, when I first entered upon the intellectual life, the irk-

[4] Written in 1937.
[5] *Of Human Bondage*, "Collected edition," v–vi.

someness of my few years at the hospital and the thrill of London.[6]

Of Human Bondage provided the release from these "teeming memories." This account of the genesis of the novel is highly significant. It explains the deep compassion, the insight into the adolescent mind, and the honesty of the book.

Of Human Bondage belongs to that type of novel which may be called "the novel of adolescence." This type of novel, which was usually represented by a long chronicle in three thick volumes and which flourished throughout the nineteenth century, had its beginning with Goethe's *Wilhelm Meister*. As has been pointed out by William Y. Tindall, this form received new life towards the end of the century from the science of biology and later from psychology.[7]

> In novel after novel sensitive lads are apprenticed to life, formed by its forces, rebelling against them, sometimes failing, sometimes emerging in victory. Their trials and errors, like those of rats in a maze, are painfully displayed. And all the horrors of adolescence, the theatre of biology and spirit, are examined. . . . From 1903 onwards almost every first novel by a serious novelist was a novel of adolescence. . . . it produced some of the best novels of the early twentieth century.[8]

Of Human Bondage is a chronicle of a period of about twenty years in the early life of Philip Carey, who is, to a large extent, Maugham himself. The opening chapter forms one of the most moving scenes in the novel. Philip's mother, who is on her deathbed, asks nine-year-old Philip to be brought to her. She presses the child, who is only half-awake, to herself, and then, "she passed her hand down his body till she came to his feet; she held the right foot in her hand and felt the five small

[6] *The Summing Up*, 130.
[7] *Forces in Modern British Literature*, 176–80.
[8] *Ibid.*, 176–77.

toes; and then slowly passed her hand over the left one. She gave a sob."[9] Thus the fact of Philip's clubfoot, which is going to cause him suffering throughout his whole life, is intimated to the reader in an effortless and effective way.

Philip's clubfoot seems to have been suggested by young Maugham's own stammer, and Maugham indeed appears to have put so much of his childhood and adolescence into the portrait of Philip that he emerges as easily the most memorable of Maugham's heroes.

Since Philip's mother dies (his father is already dead), the bringing up of the orphan is entrusted to his uncle, who is vicar of Blackstable. Philip's life at Blackstable is not happy. He is starved of affection, for his uncle is too self-centered to pay much attention to the boy; his aunt, a shy and meek childless lady, is too diffident to satisfy the boy's emotional needs. Philip's deformity, which excites ridicule and makes him exceedingly self-conscious, renders his schooldays equally unhappy. "And often there recurred to him then that queer feeling that his life with all its misery was nothing but a dream, and that he would awake in the morning in his own little bed in London."[10]

The dull routine of the school irks this dreamy and precocious boy, and he rebels against the ecclesiastical career which his uncle intends for him. However, he persuades his uncle to allow him to spend a year in Germany, where he experiences his first taste of freedom of action and thought. Still undecided about the choice of a career on his return, he spends one year in London in a chartered accountant's office, and two more in Paris, where he studies painting, until he discovers that he is devoid of genius and returns to London to become a medical student.

While Philip is pursuing his medical studies, he falls in love with Mildred, a shallow and vulgar waitress.

[9] *Of Human Bondage*, 1.   [10] *Ibid.*, 45.

He had thought of love as a rapture which seized one so that all the world seemed spring-like, he had looked forward to an ecstatic happiness, but this was not happiness; it was a hunger of the soul, it was a painful yearning, it was a bitter anguish, he had never known before.[11]

He struggles in vain against the destructive passion which robs him of his health, of his peace of mind, and of his slender financial resources. Thrice Mildred leaves his life, only to return and make fresh claims upon him. Reduced to poverty, Philip has to abandon his studies for a time and work as a shopwalker to maintain himself.

At long last, he frees himself from the cruel spell of Mildred, and, inheriting money from his uncle who has died, is able to resume his studies. He decides to travel extensively after qualifying as a doctor, but when he receives his degree, he discovers that his one desire is for peace. Throughout his adolescence and youth, one question has been nagging him— "What is the meaning of life?" He deduces that life has no meaning and that every man's life is simply a pattern that he makes out of the manifold events of his life, his deeds, his feelings, and his thoughts—a pattern that he makes simply for his own pleasure. There is "one pattern, the most obvious, perfect and beautiful, in which a man is born, grows to manhood, marries, produces children, toils for his bread, and dies." With the passing of his mental struggles, Philip decides to follow this pattern, and he marries a healthy and simple girl, settling down as a country doctor.

The appeal of *Of Human Bondage* is due, first, to the sincere desire to understand the mind of a sensitive and dreamy adolescent, secondly, to the deep sympathy with which the afflictions of this adolescent are portrayed, and, lastly, to the

11 *Ibid.*, 295.

unflinching honesty and restraint which save its compassion from sentimentality or mawkish self-pity.

The pathos of the opening scene of the novel has already been commented on. With great tenderness, Maugham portrays the sense of loneliness and desolation which haunts Philip in his early days at school. The story of how his deformity, to which he has scarcely given any thought so far, makes him woefully sensitive and self-conscious there, alienates him from the other boys, and makes him grow into a brooding, lonely, and morbid adolescent is told with great power. The career of Philip is, in broad outline, a rather depressing record of the failure of a morbid mind to adjust itself to the world and to life. Yet, it is remarkable that, throughout this long chronicle, Philip never loses our sympathy. This is perhaps due to the stark sincerity with which Maugham portrays his career, extenuating nothing and making no excuses.

The sincerity with which Maugham treats his hero is best illustrated in the Mildred episodes of the novel. Philip emerges from these episodes as an ineffectual, weak, irresolute, and drifting young man, and yet retains our sympathy. It is interesting to compare Philip's adolescent love experiences with those of Wells's Lewisham and Meredith's Richard Feverel, for both of whom adolescent love is enveloped in a rosy romantic haze. Philip, with painful honesty, confesses that "Love was like a parasite in his heart, nourishing a hateful existence on his life's blood."[12]

This sincerity is part of Maugham's creed as a realist, but it does not make him completely detached here. This is impossible, for Philip is, to a large extent, Maugham himself. On the contrary, this quality gives greater verisimilitude to the whole picture. R. H. Ward complains of a certain "rigidity" in *Of Human Bondage*, arising out of "a stubborn determination

[12] *Ibid.*, 317.

to plough right on from the beginning to the end, to extenuate nothing."[13] He thinks that this is due to the "material tyrannising over the author." But it is possible to find in this very "determination to extenuate nothing" the source of the emotional force and massiveness of the book. It is that determination, in fact, which gives unity to this sprawling and seemingly formless chronicle.

Philip is not the only object of Maugham's pity in the novel. There are the drifters through life whom Philip meets in his career, and they are pathetic spectacles—more lamentable than he in certain respects, for they are greater self-deceivers. The portraits of some of these are not devoid of irony, as for example, the picture of Hayward, who is at once the deceiver and the deceived. He has purposely impressed others as being an idealist and has led, under the cloak of idealism, an idle and wasted life. He has worn his mask so long, however, that he has ultimately come to believe in his own fiction.

Nevertheless, the dominant note in the other portraits is one of pity for waste and futility. Such is the fate of Cronshaw who is the slave of his Bohemian life in Paris, and who pitiably advises Philip, "If you can get out of it, do while there's time." Such, again, is the fate of Miss Price who, refusing to accept the fact that she has no talent for painting, blunders on through her art studies, until starvation drives her to hang herself.

Of the restraint which saves the novel from mawkish sentimentality, there is a fine example in the scene where Philip, going through the correspondence of his deceased uncle, suddenly comes upon a letter written by his mother. In that letter she writes about her son: "I pray God night and day that he may grow into a good, honest, and Christian man. . . . I hope that he will become a soldier in Christ's Faith and be all the

[13] *William Somerset Maugham* (London, 1937), 135.

days of his life God-fearing, humble, and pious." The letter moves Philip. "He read again," says Maugham, "what she said about him, what she expected and thought about him. . . . he had turned out very differently; he looked at himself for a moment."[14] And then follows a significant gesture: "Then a sudden impulse caused him to tear up the letter; its tenderness and simplicity made it seem peculiarly private. . . . He went on with the Vicar's dreary correspondence."[15]

Humanitarianism is, as noted earlier,[16] incompatible with disbelief in the sincerity or goodness of human motive and actions. Maugham, usually the ironic observer of life, has created very few men and women the goodness of whose motives and actions he does not doubt. Thorpe Athelny in *Of Human Bondage* is one of these. He is, no doubt, an absurd creature to some extent. Although he is an insignificant advertisement writer by profession, he grandiloquently calls himself "a journalist," and his garrulity and flamboyance are highly diverting. Yet with all his ridiculousness, Athelny has a pure, disarming goodness, the warmth of which is felt by all who come into contact with him. It is this goodness that succors Philip when both materially and spiritually he has reached the nadir of helplessness.

The other strain in Maugham—that of contemptuous sneering and cold indifference indicative of cynicism—also has a place in *Of Human Bondage*. It is present, first, in the unfavorable portrait of Philip's uncle, the vicar of Blackstable. Maugham is generally hard on clergymen, and in the famous short story, "Rain," in the farcical comedy *Loaves and Fishes* and elsewhere in his work, clergymen are butts of ridicule. The Vicar of Blackstable is a detestable creature both as a clergy-

14 *Of Human Bondage*, 593.
15 *Ibid.*, 593.
16 Chap. i, part ii.

man and as a man. He is self-centered, vain, mean, avaricious, and indolent. Maugham takes delight in exposing him through small situations. Thus, when the Vicar and his wife play back-gammon, the wife always arranges that he should win, because he is a bad loser. But it is when the Vicar is about to die that Maugham's satire becomes most stinging. Far from reconciling himself to the thought of joining his Maker after a life spent in ease and comfort, this man of God has become a valetudi-narian monster, clinging desperately to existence. The thought of death fills him with horror, and the religion that he has preached all his life is now of no avail to him.

But the attack on the clergy and religion in *Of Human Bondage* has more of contemptuous sneering and frigid in-difference than of indignation in it. John Brophy makes an illuminating comparison between Samuel Butler's *The Way of All Flesh* and *Of Human Bondage* from this point of view: "*The Way of All Flesh* is inspired by violent anger against the clergy because they offended Butler's moral sense. The hypocrisy reported in *Of Human Bondage* arouses not so much indigna-tion as distaste." Thus, when Philip loses his faith, he does so

> ... with surprise at the foolishness of believers, but with no sense of shock, no moral indignation. Convinced that religion is nonsense, he feels no obligation to disabuse others of what he regards as mere fantasy, even when he observes that on their death-beds it fails to console them. Maugham notes, as it were, in a casebook: this man is dying of pneumonia because, curious creature, he insists on going out in the rain. The fact is reported and the comment added without passion, without even con-cern. Samuel Butler, by contrast, professes social medicine. He is appalled that the contagion should be spread. He denounces religion in a satire so hot that it scorches and discomforts not only the object of his scorn but the reader and himself. He would have the churches pulled down and sterlized, and he has

already planned the temples to the Life Force which should be built in their place.[17]

This is, indeed, the reason why *Of Human Bondage* misses the greatness which its rich compassion for Philip brings it near attaining. The deep sensibility and honesty of the book are undeniable, but it fails to attain greatness because of what R. H. Ward rightly describes as its "negative quality." *Of Human Bondage* has," he says, "one great disadvantage, that it is written by a man determined that only thought and the material, with the material as leader and ruler exist. It is, as a result, a good book, but an un-illumined book."[18]

The negativeness of *Of Human Bondage* lies mainly in the solution which Maugham ultimately has his protagonist find to the question: "What is the meaning of life?" The conclusion arrived at by Philip is, "There was no meaning in life, and man by living served no end. It was immaterial whether he was born or not born, whether he lived or ceased to live."[19] Philip's reaction to this conclusion is even more revealing:

> Philip exulted, as he had exulted in his boyhood when the weight of a belief in God was lifted from his shoulders; it seemed to him that the last burden of responsibility was taken from him; and for the first time he was utterly free . . . what he did or left undone did not matter. Failure was unimportant and success amounted to nothing.[20]

The total lack of positive values in Philip's creed is self-evident. He no doubt speaks, later on, about every man making "a pattern of his life for his own pleasure," and tells us that "there was one pattern, the most obvious, perfect and beautiful,

---

[17] *Somerset Maugham,* "The British Council Bibliographical Series," 1952, pp. 17–18.
[18] W. *Somerset Maugham,* 134.
[19] *Of Human Bondage,* 559.
[20] *Ibid.,* 559.

in which a man was born, grew to manhood, married, produced children, toiled for his bread, and died."[21] But it is significant that the end of the novel where Philip chooses this pattern for his own life is, according to most critics, the least satisfactory part of the book. Maugham himself mentions this in his preface to *Of Human Bondage* and is almost apologetic about it: "Here," he says, "I had no facts to go on. It was a wish-fulfilment."[22] The fact is that Philip's sudden apprehension of this perfect pattern is not well prepared for in his psychological portraiture and lacks adequate motivation. Hence it fails to convince. It must also be remembered that Maugham's philosophy of life, as stated in *The Summing Up*, also shows an almost total lack of a positive creed.[23]

The negativeness of *Of Human Bondage* is no doubt mitigated to a considerable extent by its author's humanitarianism, by the fundamental honesty of the book, and by the goodness discernible in Athelny. Nevertheless, it cuts too deep into the work to be wholly dissipated by these and is especially emphasized, as shown earlier, in the concluding portions of the novel.

The dominant strain in *Of Human Bondage* is that of understanding and compassion: "I was not writing to please, I was writing to free myself of an intolerable obsession," says Maugham in commenting on the genesis of the book.[24] Hence, the transparent sincerity of the work and the human warmth pervading the struggles and trials of adolescent Philip are explained.

The novel has many faults. It is too long and verbose, and the ending where Philip is thrown hastily into Sally's arms is rather hard to swallow, if not disgusting. From the point of

21 *Ibid.*, 560.
22 *Ibid.*, vi.
23 Chapter XII.
24 *Of Human Bondage*, v.

view of form, the novel is indeed only a sprawling chronicle such as a panoramic novel usually is, and, like other lengthy chronicles, it has its redundancies and repetitions. But the greatest limitation of the book is its negativeness of philosophy which persists, though mitigated to a point by other elements in the novel. Yet, in spite of all these shortcomings, the humanitarianism of *Of Human Bondage*, which is undeniable, effectively counterbalances its strain of cynicism. The tables, however, are turned with Maugham's next novel, *The Moon and Sixpence*.

CHAPTER FIVE

The Middle Phase

·

HAVING FINISHED *Of Human Bondage,* Maugham began preparing, as he wrote in *The Summing Up,* "to make a fresh start."[1] *The Moon and Sixpence* was the first fruit of this "fresh start" and of a different style of writing which was generally called the characteristic "Maugham-manner." This manner can be described as a detached, amused, and ironical attitude towards the world and life, in which the author repressed his sympathies and contemplated the spectacle of existence with an indifferent shrug. It dominated the whole of the middle phase of Maugham's literary career.[2]

An essential feature of the Maugham-manner was the method of narration that Maugham employed for the first time in *The Moon and Sixpence,* which later became his favorite mode of narration both in the novels and the short stories—the narration in the first person, where the author himself was a character in the story, though he played a minor role. The role that he filled was one of an onlooker reporting on the major characters and their actions. This method of narration had obvious advantages for the Maugham-manner.

The Moon and Sixpence has both the new method of nar-

---

[1] *The Summing Up,* 131.
[2] Novels: *The Moon and Sixpence* (1919) and *The Painted Veil* (1925). Plays: *Our Betters* (written 1915, published 1923); *The Unknown* (1920); *The Circle* (1921); *Caesar's Wife* (1922); *East of Suez* (1922); *Home and the Beauty* (1923); *The Unattainable* (1923); *The Constant Wife* (1927).

ration and the new outlook on life. Its theme is the mystery of genius. The novel sketches the career of Charles Strickland, a commonplace and dull English stockbroker, who, when he is fat and forty, is suddenly obsessed by an overwhelming desire to become an artist. He abandons his business and his family; he paints in Paris and nearly starves; he sacrifices everything— his friends, his better feelings, even decency—to his art. After having dreamed of a lonely island where he can find what he wants, he fulfils his dream by traveling to Tahiti, where he paints his best pictures, but finally dies of leprosy.

Strickland was obviously suggested by Paul Gauguin (1848–1903), in whom, too, the pursuit of art awakened a ferocious egoism. He also was lured by the beauty of the South Seas, but he died of syphilis rather than of Hansen's disease.

Paris was beginning to discover Gauguin just after World War I, and Maugham, who, after having written *Of Human Bondage* to please himself, had decided henceforth to have his finger on the pulse of the public, immediately wrote *The Moon and Sixpence.*

The theme—the mystery of genius—is treated in a peculiar way. Maugham makes no attempt to fathom the mystery of Strickland's character, of the sudden change in him, or of what he had hoped to achieve. There is no motive-hunting at all, only a plain, unvarnished, straightforward narrative. Strickland, as a man, is portrayed as a selfish, brutal, and callous egoist, who is almost outside the pale of what is human. The only explanation given for his behavior is that he is a genius—a man under the spell of the creative instinct, which makes him thoroughly indifferent to all human values and which does not allow him to rest until he has given it its due.

Time and again, Maugham breaks in with an almost disarmingly frank confession of his ignorance of Strickland's motives and of his inability to fathom the riddle of genius. He employs a variety of devices to secure verisimilitude. He insists that he is writing a biography and not a novel, and the opening pages are cluttered with an imposing array of footnotes which refer to the critical and biographical works which were supposed to have been written on Strickland and his pictures. These stock devices, already used to so fine effect by Swift in *Gulliver's Travels* and by Defoe in *Robinson Crusoe*, do not fail, but they do suggest that Maugham has merely fenced with his problem in *The Moon and Sixpence* rather than faced it boldly.

The casual reader may be satisfied with Maugham's clever harping upon the idea that the riddle of Strickland's mind has no clue, but the discerning reader is probably troubled by the disquieting thought that Maugham makes Strickland such a mystery either because he does not wish to take the time and trouble to explain his riddle or because (and this is a more disturbing thought) the author is emotionally incapable of doing so. The point may be illustrated by a comparison. Hamlet is as much of a mystery as Strickland, and so is Cleopatra. In fact, it is this complexity, this unexpectedness that is the true mark of a great character in literature. The difference, however, between Strickland on the one hand, and Hamlet and Cleopatra on the other is that the two creations of Shakespeare are unfathomable, yet they stir our emotions so deeply and are so intensely human that we at once feel that we know them, we have always known them, and yet in a sense we do not and never shall. It would be rash to make the same claim for Strickland.

The shallowness of Strickland's character probably lies with the method that Maugham employed to depict the mystery of Strickland's mind. He surrendered the novelist's privilege of omniscience and resorted to the limited view of the narrator who is the observer of the phenomenon under consideration. It would be impossible for a casual acquaintance of Strickland to know the "in's" and "out's" of his character, and the result is that the detached, amused observer of the mystery of genius produces a very interesting story, but being outside, he can do no more. Strickland does not stir our sympathies deeply, because he does not seem to have stirred Maugham's.

The character of Dick Stroeve is another example of how Maugham seems to have been bent on repressing his sympathies in *The Moon and Sixpence*. Dick Stroeve may indeed be called Maugham's revenge upon his emotional self. He is a peculiar character and, in the author's own words, "one of those persons whom, according to your character, you cannot think of without derisive laughter or an embarrassed shrug of the shoulders."[3] He is fat and foolish, naïve and grotesque, sheepish and absurd, and a very poor artist. Yet, we are told, he is good and kind-hearted, generous and unselfish, and a very sound judge of art. But with all his goodness, Dick Stroeve does not arouse our sympathies. The contrast between his character and that of Thorpe Athelny in *Of Human Bondage* is highly significant. The latter, too, is a kindly soul who is thoroughly ridiculous. Yet he claims Maugham's sympathy and ours too—Stroeve does not. The difference is suggestive of the change in Maugham.

In *The Moon and Sixpence* appear, for the first time, the cynical obiter dicta which, too, are an essential part of the typical Maugham-manner. In the opening pages, Maugham takes his characteristic fling at the clergy, when he brings his polished irony into play against the Reverend Robert Strickland who has depicted his father, the artist, as an angel of domestic propriety in the *Life of Charles Strickland*. But this is playful banter if compared with the sundry observations on the world and human life which are scattered throughout the novel. Of course, the "I" of the narrator need not necessarily be Maugham himself, but, henceforth, whenever Maugham employs this method of narration, whether in the novel or in the short story, the nar-

3 *The Moon and Sixpence*, 87.

rator has a peculiar outlook on life—that of the detached, amused, ironical observer, which may therefore be regarded as being characteristic of the author himself.

This is how he feels about moral indignation: "I am a little shy of any assumption of moral indignation. There is always in it an element of self-satisfaction which makes it awkward to anyone who has a sense of humour."[4] Of emotion he remarks: "Do we not know that man in moments of emotion expresses himself naturally in the terms of a novelette?"[5] As for conscience, we are told that:

> Conscience is the guardian in the individual of the rules which the community has evolved for its own preservation. Man's desire for the approval of his fellows is so strong, his dread of their censure so violent, that he himself has brought his enemy within his gates.[6]

And again:

> Sympathy is a charming faculty, but one often abused by those who are conscious of its possession: for there is something ghoulish in the avidity with which they will pounce upon the misfortune of their friends so that they may exercise their dexterity. It gushes forth like an oil-well.[7]

Woman, the eternal butt of the cynic and the satirist, gets more than her due.

> I did not then know the besetting sin of woman, the passion to discuss her private affairs with anyone who is willing to listen.[8]
> I did not know then how great a part is played in women's lives by the opinions of others. It throws a shadow of insincerity over their most deeply felt emotions.[9]

[4] *Ibid.*, 161.
[5] *Ibid.*, 189.
[6] *Ibid.*, 72–79.
[7] *Ibid.*, 22.
[8] *Ibid.*, 38.
[9] *Ibid.*, 48.

Lastly, of great interest is the confession that the narrator (who evidently represents Maugham) makes about the writer's calling:

> Until long habit has blunted the sensibility, there is something disconcerting to the writer in the instinct which causes him to take an interest in the singularities of human nature so absorbing that his moral sense is powerless against it. . . . The character of a scoundrel has a fascination for his creator which is an outrage to law and order. . . . It may be that in his rogues the writer gratifies instincts deep-rooted in him. . . . His satisfaction is a sense of liberation.[10]

From *The Moon and Sixpence* onwards, Maugham enjoys this satisfaction to his heart's content. The passage quoted above ends with a significant remark: "The writer is more concerned to know than to judge"—this may almost be said to be Maugham's motto in this phase of his work. But Maugham forgets that to observe in a detached, ironical manner is only to see and not to apprehend. To know is to forget detachment, to sympathize, to understand, to praise and to blame, to condemn, and to forgive. The reader of *The Moon and Sixpence*, therefore, does not get to know Strickland, but merely observes him from the outside as Strickland's creator does. Thus, the chief limitation of the "fresh start" made by Maugham in this novel is immediately revealed.

The Painted Veil (1925), Maugham's next novel, shows the fresh start duly followed up with only one point of difference, the narration reverts to the third person. The story was suggested, as Maugham explains in the preface, by a passage in Dante's *Inferno* which tells of Pia, a gentlewoman of Siena, whose husband, suspecting her of adultery but afraid to put her to death because of her family, took her to his castle in the Maremma, where the noxious vapors, he was confident, would

[10] *Ibid.*, 195.

soon kill her; when the vapors failed, he had her thrown from a window.

Maugham gives the story a modern setting. His Pia-Kitty, a frivolous, pleasure-loving girl, has married Walter Fane, a young bacteriologist stationed in China, not because she loves him, but because it is high time she got married. She develops a passion for Charles Townsend, the assistant colonial secretary, an equally frivolous extrovert, and yields to him. The husband, who learns of the intrigue, decides to punish her by taking her to a place ravaged by an epidemic, where he volunteers to go on duty. By a strange stroke of irony it is he who dies. Kitty, full of remorse, despises her lover, yet yields to him again. Finally, we are told that her remorse is genuine and deep and that she leaves determined to start life afresh.

There is enough material in this theme for a soul-stirring tragedy of crime and punishment. *The Painted Veil*, however, is little more than a sordid tale of rather common passion. The reason is close at hand. *The Painted Veil* is not a tragedy, because it is difficult to sympathize with any of the major characters in the book. Kitty has hardly a single redeeming trait in her character, and even her love for Townsend is nothing but animal passion.

It is interesting to contrast Kitty with Bertha, the heroine of *Mrs. Craddock*. Both are victims of passion, but Bertha contends with passion, and her struggle is almost heroic. In the snobbish, self-indulgent, weak, and sensual Kitty there is no struggle but only abject surrender. Moreover, Bertha's passion is a thirst of the soul, whereas Kitty's appears to be mere animal desire. Bertha's tribulations are, therefore, on a much higher level than those of Kitty. Suffering chastens Bertha. It is difficult to believe the same about Kitty. At the conclusion of *The Painted Veil*, the author tells us of Kitty's remorse and her desire to turn over a new leaf, but there is nothing in Kitty's character to warrant that this gross, worldly creature will ever be able to break the chains of sensuality which bind her.

Charles Townsend the lover is the male counterpart of Kitty. A vain, self-seeking, weak, and cowardly individual, Townsend's conception of love is mere sexual congress.

Strangely enough, it is also difficult to sympathize with the injured husband. Walter Fane is a thoroughly unsympathetic portrait. He is the sentimentalist-turned-cynic, a type on which Maugham is particularly hard, probably because in it he finds something of himself. Walter is shy, self-conscious, and emotional, yet, afraid of emotion. He conceals his feelings under a cold, sarcastic, tight-lipped exterior. Maugham speaks about "his extreme sensitiveness for which his acid irony was a protection."[11] Walter is another victim of Maugham's detached, ironical attitude.

Although Maugham does not employ the method of narration in the first person, he still forgoes his right to omniscience. He makes no attempt to examine Walter's heart or to reveal the aching soul of his reserved protagonist. What Walter feels when he realizes the perfidy of his wife and decides to punish her in that strange fashion is as much of a mystery to us as to Kitty. Nor is Walter's death, the irony of which makes his cynical self chuckle, calculated to arouse any sympathy for him.

The role of the detached narrator is filled by Waddington, the customs officer, who is made to watch the drama of Kitty and her husband when they go to the plague-stricken city. Waddington is another projection of the cynical propensities in Maugham. "He seemed to look upon life," we are told, "in a spirit of banter, and his ridicule . . . was acid. . . . He could not tell a tragic story or one of heroism without making it faintly absurd."[12] He is a shrewd, cool, ironical observer of life. Yet,

[11] *The Painted Veil*, 195.
[12] *Ibid.*, 119.

like most cynics, he is a sentimentalist at heart. He is deeply attached to a Manchu woman of noble blood who has sacrificed everything for his sake, and he has his moments of mysticism, when he talks eloquently about "the way and waygoer and the eternal road along which walk all beings, but no being made it, for itself is being [but only when, as he himself puts it] I've had half a dozen whiskies and look at the stars."[13]

To sum up, *The Painted Veil* leaves a disquieting impression. It is a book that does not escape the taint of gross earthiness, and the fault, at least partly, must rest with Maugham's cynical self which has now begun to predominate over his sympathies.

The middle phase of Maugham's dramatic activity begins with *Our Betters* (written in 1915) and ends with *The Constant Wife* (1927). This is how Maugham describes the eight plays[14] which he wrote during this period:

> They were written in the tradition which flourished so brightly in the Restoration Period, which was carried on by Goldsmith and Sheridan, and which, since it has had so long a vogue, may be supposed to have something in it that peculiarly appeals to the English temper. . . . It is drama not of action, but of conversation. It treats with indulgent cynicism the humours, follies and vices of the world of fashion. It is urbane, sentimental at times, for that is in the English character, and a trifle unreal. It does not preach: Sometimes it draws a moral, but with a shrug of shoulders as if to invite you to lay no too great stress on it.[15]

But the plays in this group are not all cut from the same bolt of material. There is ample variety here. *Our Betters, The Circle,* and *The Constant Wife* represent the comedy of manners and morals. *The Unknown* is an example of the drama of

[13] *Ibid.,* 234.
[14] Listed in footnote 1.
[15] *The Summing Up,* 82–83.

ideas, a type of which Maugham strongly disapproves in *The Summing Up*; *Home and Beauty* and *The Unattainable* are farces; *East of Suez* and *Caesar's Wife* are attempts to master the costume play.

Our Betters and its two companion pieces depict the change from *Penelope* (1912) and *Smith* (1913) of Maugham's first dramatic phase to stronger satire, which occasionally became cynicism. It is an advance from the comedy of manners to the comedy of morals. This is specially marked in *Our Betters*, which Allardyce Nicoll rightly describes as "pure Wycherley."[16]

It is a somber picture of the aristocratic English society that emerges from this play. It is a world that brazenly worships Pan and Mammon and then prides itself on its culture and elegance; a world peopled by shameless sensualists, snobs and self-deceivers, idlers, parasites, painted old ladies with their kept boys, and young ladies who barter millions in marriage vows (which they never dream of keeping) to impoverished lords for a title. Chastity is a social disgrace, and to have any scruples is cowardly. Bessie Saunders, the rich American heiress who is about to settle down in this setting, realizes in time the futility and rottenness of the lives of the rich Americans who, upon entering this milieu, have lost one code and fail to find another.

It is illuminating to compare *Our Betters* with *Smith*. In the earlier play, as has been shown,[17] the positive values are stressed time and again through Freeman, who is a newcomer to the fashionable world. What Freeman is to *Smith*, the young Americans Fleming and Bessie are to the latter play. They are not, however, given as much latitude as Freeman. Then again, Rose, the center of the corrupt world of fashion in *Smith*, is only a slight sketch as compared with Pearl who dominates *Our Betters*. Pearl the callous, unscrupulous, and cynical society

16 *British Drama*, 469.
17 Chap. iii.

belle, is false, and brazenly so. *Our Betters*, therefore, is almost savage satire if compared with *Smith* and shows definite touches of cynicism.

The theme of *The Circle*, commonly believed to be Maugham's best play, is that in love every couple has to face its problems alone. The experiences of others do not help. The wheel comes full circle, but no lessons can be drawn from its movement. So, Mrs. Elizabeth Champion-Cheney runs away with Edward Luton knowing that Lady Kitty and Lord Porteous have ruined their lives by eloping. The theme is really tragic, but its tragical possibilities are not developed, except for the pathos of the incident in Act III, where the old lovers, realizing the waste of their existence, forgive each other. Maugham creates a sardonic comedy with the old lovers. In an almost brutal way he reveals the depths to which they sink, and how love dies and only leaves behind a sordid record of two frivolous, wasted lives. To avoid any suggestion of tragedy, he makes Arnold, the husband of Elizabeth, a thoroughly cold prig and thus incapable of winning our sympathy. *The Circle* has sparkling wit, unity of idea, compactness of construction, and a highly effective stroke of irony at the end. But the prevailing mood is sardonic.

The Constant Wife, the last play of this trio, is the *Penelope* of this phase of Maugham's work. But it is so with a difference. Both plays have a frank air of intellectualism, but *The Constant Wife* has a cold cynicism which is absent in *Penelope*. Its subject is marriage among well-to-do people, and the conclusions drawn by the heroine are startling: The wife of an upper-middle-class man is only an expensive toy which he buys at the altar where alone it can conveniently be purchased, and so no better than a parasite. The husband has every reason to be unfaithful to her, for men are by nature polygamous. The wife, however, must remain faithful to her spouse because she

eats his bread. If, however, the wife can secure economic freedom for herself, she, too, can scorn chastity and be none the
worse for it.

Sentiment is carefully kept out of the play, and the atmosphere of cold rationalism does not allow its cynicism to become
bitter. Yet cynicism is unmistakably there in spite of the sparkling wit of the play and the pure comedy of the scenes where
the constant wife scores over her husband and the lady with
whom he is flirting.

Caesar's Wife and *East of Suez* are plays of spectacle, the
background in the first being that of exotic Egypt and in the
second, one of a colorful Chinese city. *Caesar's Wife* was suggested by Madame de Lafayette's novel *La Princesse de Clèves*.
The plot is as follows:

> Monsieur de Clèves had fallen in love with his wife at first
> sight, but was aware that she had for him no more than affec-
> tion; but his respect and admiration for her were so great that
> when, inviting his aid in her distress, she told him that she loved
> another, he accepted her confession with sympathy. The drama
> lies in the effort of Monsieur de Clèves to overcome his jealousy
> and in his wife's to master her passion.[18]

Commenting on the novel, Maugham said:

> It is beautiful to see the skill with which Madame de Lafay-
> ette depicts the gradual disintegration of this great gentleman's
> character. The situation is unfolded with sobriety . . . and the
> expression of the most violent emotion is kept within the
> bounds of propriety. But the emotion is deep and true.[19]

Unfortunately, all this cannot be said of Maugham's play.
First, the tragic degeneration in the husband is almost absent
in Maugham's portrayal, because the husband here is a pillar of

[18] *Collected Plays*, Vol. III, p. vii.
[19] *Ibid.*, Vol. III, p. vii.

the British Empire and is shown to be incapable of degeneration. Moreover, the struggle in the hearts of the husband and the erring wife is too slightly sketched. Hence, what should have been a tragic drama full of intense conflict and deep emotion is only an exotic costume play. Once more, Maugham shys away from sentiment and pays the price.

East of Suez lies open to the same charge as the novel, *The Painted Veil*, viz., sordidness, arising out of the author's inability to win our sympathies for any single character in the story. Here again, the theme was rich in tragical possibilities— the predicament of the Eurasian who finds himself "between two worlds," to neither of which he can wholly belong. But there is no character in the play which is not thoroughly odious —whether Daisy, the Eurasian, who is a composite of the worst traits in the two cultures, or George Conway, her weak lover, or Lee Tai Chang, the crafty and unscrupulous Chinaman. In spite of its colorful background, the play leaves an unpleasant taste in the mouth.

The Unknown, the last of the plays to be considered from this phase of Maugham's work, is a play of ideas—probably the only definite example of its kind in Maugham's output. The problem is the loss of faith and its effect on a young couple engaged to be married. But, as Maugham confessed:

> ... the drama I saw in my mind's eye lay in the conflict between two persons who loved one another and were divided by the simple piety of the one and the lost faith of the other. But to my surprise it appeared in the representation that the drama lay in the arguments on one side and the other, and not at all in the personal relations of the characters.[20]

The result is that neither John's loss of faith nor the struggle between faith and love in Sylvia is portrayed powerfully enough.

[20] *Collected Plays*, Vol. II, pp. xvi–xvii.

Both are treated as almost theoretical propositions, and the play consequently lacks human warmth. Maugham complained in *The Summing Up* that the demand for the play of ideas "is responsible for the lamentable decadence of our theatre."[21] It is fortunate that he made no further contributions to this "lamentable decadence." *Home and Beauty* and *The Unattainable*, pleasant farces full of horseplay, fun, and absurdity, and revealing the lighter side of Maugham's comic muse, need not detain us.

The middle phase of Maugham's work reveals a distinct change from the prevailing mood of the early phase and *Of Human Bondage*. There the native sensibility of Maugham was strong and active, and kept his ironic and cynical propensities in check. The "fresh start" made in *The Moon and Sixpence* illustrates Maugham's ironic self progressively getting the upper hand. The cynical obiter dicta of this novel make Miss Ley's ironic comments in *Mrs. Craddock* appear as mere innocuous pleasantries, and the callousness of *The Painted Veil* is unimaginable in Bertha's chronicle.

The same process is seen at work in the plays of this phase. Maugham turns from the gay, irresponsible comedy of manners to the sardonic comedy of social satire. His satire becomes sharper and his laughter is often a bitter grimace. The reason for this is that the positive values so insistently kept in sight throughout the comedies of the early phase are but faintly, if at all, indicated here, and not all of their intellectualism and artificiality (which are often cited in their defense) can hide the element of cynicism in these plays.

The results of the dominance of Maugham's ironic self and the suppression of his sympathies in this phase are not happy. There is here, it must be admitted, a distinct and major advance in technique. The compactness of both *The Moon and Sixpence*

21 *The Summing Up*, 93.

and *The Painted Veil* contrasts favorably with the sprawling verbosity of *Mrs. Craddock* and *Of Human Bondage*. In the plays, too, the dialogue attains greater crispness and sparkle. The management of comic situation in *The Constant Wife* is a triumph, and *The Circle* reaches a perfection of form which shows that Maugham has now attained complete mastery over dramatic technique. But technical perfection alone is not enough. In book after book of this phase, Maugham, bent on repressing his sympathies, seems wilfully to sacrifice the emotional possibilities of his themes. The results are disastrous. Maugham only succeeds in creating plots which are amusing and interesting, but nothing more.

The mischief, however, does not stop here. The detached, indifferent, and ironic attitude toward life which Maugham carefully cultivates during this phase soon becomes a habit. It is no doubt very useful in the treatment of certain themes. But when, in his last phase, Maugham, growing more serious, seeks to delve deeper into life and grapple with its eternal problems, this attitude which has now become native is seen to become a definite handicap. Before this happens, Maugham's sensibility, fighting back, registers one more triumph in *Cakes and Ale*. It is, however, a victory followed by a disastrous relapse.

CHAPTER SIX

Cakes and Ale

.

C HRONOLOGICALLY, *Cakes and Ale*[1] stands at the center of Maugham's literary career. It may also be said to stand midway among his novels from another point of view, for here the two strains in Maugham, viz., cynicism and humanitarianism, are in perfect balance. As has been shown in chapter five, with the beginning of the middle phase of Maugham's work, the former strain had begun to overshadow the latter. In *Cakes and Ale*, however, Maugham's sensibility wells up strong and pure and creates what is probably his best and most sympathetically created female character—Rosie. On the other hand, in the literary world described in the novel, Maugham's polished cynicism revels to its heart's desire. Thus, both of the twin selves in Maugham fulfill themselves completely in *Cakes and Ale*, and that is probably why it is Maugham's most characteristic work.

The genesis of *Cakes and Ale*, as narrated by Maugham in his preface to the novel, makes interesting reading. He first thought of the novel as "a short story, and not a very long one either"; and the note he made of the plot was:

> I am asked to write my reminiscences of a famous novelist, a friend of my boyhood, living at W., with a common wife, very unfaithful to him. There he writes his great books. Later he marries his secretary, who guards him and makes him into a

[1] *Cakes and Ale, or The Skeleton in the Cupboard* (1930).

figure. My wonder whether even in old age he is not slightly restive at being made into a monument.²

Maugham continues:

> As my note suggests I had been struck by the notion that the veneration to which an author full of years and honour is exposed must be irksome to the little alert soul within him that is alive still to the adventures of his fancy. Many old and disconcerting ideas must cross his mind, I thought, while he maintains the dignified exterior that his admirers demand of him.³

With this theme Maugham combined another—the character of a nymphomaniac. "I had long had in mind," he continues, "the character of Rosie. I had wanted for years to write about her, but the opportunity never presented itself; I could contrive no setting in which she found a place to suit her and I began to think I never should."⁴ By a happy stroke of inspiration, he made her the wife of the famous novelist.

As he tells us, Maugham thought of writing with this material a long short-story like "Rain," but he did not want, as he put it, "to waste my Rosie on a story even of this length." It was another happy inspiration to return to Blackstable, to his boyhood there, and to his uncle and aunt; "the Philip Carey of the earlier book [i.e., *Of Human Bondage*] became the 'I' of *Cakes and Ale*."⁵

Cakes and Ale, or *The Skeleton in the Cupboard,* as its double title suggests, thus came to have a twofold theme. The first, indicated by the title *Cakes and Ale,* (taken from Sir Toby Belch's famous defense of his way of life—"Dost thou think,

2 *Ibid.,* v.
3 *Ibid.,* vii.
4 *Ibid.,* vi.
5 *Ibid.,* vi.

because thou art virtuous there shall be no more cakes and ale?") is, in fact, a defense of Rosie, the nymphomaniac. The second, suggested by the subtitle, *The Skeleton in Cupboard*, centers round the novelist Driffield, whose real self is stifled under the trappings of his fame and honor. The two themes are deftly woven together, and the novel is a model of construction.

The method of narration is the same as in *The Moon and Sixpence*, viz., narration by a detached observer who plays a part in the story. He appears here as Mr. Ashenden, a novelist. The novel opens with Alroy Kear, a young and successful novelist who has come to meet Ashenden. Edward Driffield, who has achieved a legendary fame as a novelist in his old age, is dead, and Kear has been commissioned by Mrs. Driffield to write the authorized biography of her husband. Ashenden in his early life has had the privilege to come into contact with Driffield, and hence Kear requests him to offer his impressions of the great man's personality. Ashenden's mind is crowded with memories of the past, of Driffield's early struggles, and of the sweetness of the character of his first wife, Rosie. The truth about Driffield, which in no way does credit to the legendary figure, is most unpalatable for Kear and the second Mrs. Driffield, but Ashenden, determined to reveal "the skeleton in the cupboard," does so mercilessly.

The part of *Cakes and Ale* which deals with the literary world and its shams is replete with irony and sarcasm, which occasionally shade off into cynicism. The very opening is characteristic:

> I have noticed that when some one asks for you on the telephone and, finding you out, leaves a message begging you to call him up the moment you come in, and it's important, the matter is more often important to him than to you. When it comes to making you a present or doing you a favour most people are able to hold their impatience within reasonable bounds.

The very first chapter gives a highly sarcastic account of the career and the methods of the young popular novelist, Alroy Kear. When *Cakes and Ale* was first published, gossip identified Kear with Hugh Walpole. But Maugham tells us in the preface to the reprint of the novel in the "Collected Edition," that Kear was:

> . . . a composite portrait. . . . I took the appearance from one writer, the obsession with good society from another, the heartiness from a third, the pride in athletic prowess from a fourth, and a great deal of myself. For I have a grim capacity for seeking my own absurdity and I find in myself much to excite my ridicule.[6]

Whatever its sources, the composite portrait of Kear is steeped in caustic irony. He is a writer who has made a science of winning fame and popularity by methods which are subtle and not above board. His native talent is so small that "like the wise man's daily dose of Bemax," it "might have gone into a heaped-up tablespoon."[7] Yet his methods carry him far.

He trims his sails to the changing winds of popular fashion, sincerely believing "what everyone else believed at that moment."[8] By subtle flattery of the older writers and the critics, he secures favorable reviews for his books. He brutally drops former friends when they cease to be of use to him. When he lectures on his contemporaries, he "damns them with faint praise," and thus indirectly boosts up his own stock. He meddles with every organization even remotely connected with literature, in order to keep himself "in the picture." Thus does Kear climb the ladder of fame with methodical ruthlessness. Maugham concludes the sketch with a stinging comment: "He was an example of what an author can do, and to what heights he can rise, by

[6] *Ibid.*, viii.
[7] *Ibid.*, 3.
[8] *Ibid.*, 14.

industry, common sense, honesty, and the efficient combination of means and ends."

Although Kear is an interesting study, he is not Maugham's main concern in the novel. In the portrayal of Edward Driffield's literary career, which is one of the two main themes of the novel, Maugham sardonically analyzes the process by which an author wins fame. It is not the sterling qualities of his work that makes an author a classic. For this, he must live sufficiently long to be made into a living legend. Then he becomes the Grand Old Man of letters and is admired, respected, worshipped, and no longer read. In short, longevity is genius, especially in England. Thus, "who but the English would fill Covent Garden to listen to an aged prima donna without a voice?"[9] Because, for Englishmen, at an age when a man would be too old to be a clerk, or a gardener, or a magistrate, he is ripe to govern the country.

Driffield at the age of sixty is only a passable author of talent, but as soon as he celebrates his seventieth birthday, an uneasiness passes over the world of letters. Critics and the cultured begin to suspect faintly that he has genius. His works are reprinted in complete and select and a thousand other editions, and enthusiastically dissected by critics and journalists. When Driffield becomes seventy-five years old, it becomes a truism that he is a genius; at eighty he duly becomes the Grand Old Man of English letters.

It is the second Mrs. Driffield who creates with prodigious industry the imposing Driffield legend. The old man has certain habits which are not quite seemly in the Grand Old Man of letters—such as his aversion to taking a bath, his habit of mixing freely with the riff-raff of the village, and his unscrupulousness in money matters. Mrs. Driffield strives to make a gentleman of him, much to the discomfort and annoyance of

[9] *Ibid.*, 124.

the poor man. It is much easier for her to make him a museum piece after his death. This she does with great thoroughness. An example of her method of creating the Driffield legend is provided by the fact that she replaces the "horrible old desk," at which Driffield has written his best books and to which he is greatly attached, with an artistic period piece, which she proudly exhibits as her husband's writing desk.

Edward Driffield is generally thought to be a satire on Thomas Hardy, between whose life and career and Driffield's there are at least some points of resemblance. Maugham, however, stoutly denied the suggestion. Hardy, he said, "was no more in my mind than Meredith or Anatole France."[10] The Hardians are not quite convinced, and we find C. J. Weber complaining against "this sort of mischievous fiction"[11] in the Hardy centenary volume, *Hardy of Wessex* (1940).

Whatever the truth, the fact remains that Maugham's picture of Driffield's fame and literary reputation in *Cakes and Ale*, at least at certain places, all its legitimate irony conceded, savors of cynicism. Such, for example, is Maugham's analysis of Driffield's genius. For here again, the one-sidedness of the picture is self-evident, and it has already been shown how, when Maugham tries to show the other side of the shield in Charles Strickland (*The Moon and Sixpence*), the attempt is a total failure.

Maugham exposes many other shams in the literary world. He has another fling at literary fame in the picture of Jasper Gibbons, the poet, who wakes up one fine morning to find himself famous. Critics quarrel bitterly over the question as to which of them discovered him. Another not-so-fine morning he finds himself out of fashion. Critics tear him to pieces, and friends drop him with much tact and sympathy, but with haste.

[10] *Ibid.*, vii.
[11] Pages 156–57.

Allgood Newton, the celebrated critic, who flatters authors to their faces and is malicious behind their backs, is another of Maugham's immortalized shams. There is, again, Mrs. Barton Trafford, that cultured little lady who has a passion for making literary lions her domestic pets. As soon as an author shows promise, Mrs. Barton Trafford showers on him her infinite sympathy, understanding, and encouragement, and one more addition is made to her menagerie. No one, however, can be more tactful than she, when one of these lions turns out to be only a mewing creature of the lower feline order. He is then dropped, but dropped like "gentle rain from heaven upon the place beneath."

On the whole, the irony and sarcasm of *Cakes and Ale* are mellowed down, except at certain places, in the picture of Driffield's glory. The explanation for this is provided by the second theme of the novel—the character of Rosie—which fascinates Maugham so much, that his sympathy for her permeates the whole book, saving its irony from becoming cynical. Maugham's irony is never so playful and vivacious as in that fine passage where he suggests that "now that the House of Lords must inevitably in a short while be abolished, it would be a very good plan if the profession of literature were by law confined to its members,"[12] as a graceful compensation to the peers. He details how the different provinces of literature could be apportioned among the various ranks of the nobility—the earls, for example, writing only fiction, because "they have already shown their aptitude for this difficult art."

Rosie Driffield is one of the three women created by Maugham whom he viewed with so much sympathy and understanding that the reader, too, is compelled to do the same—the other two being Liza and Bertha Craddock.

It was not an easy task to enlist the reader's sympathy for

[12] *Cakes and Ale*, 159–61.

Rosie, for she is an abnormal woman, a nymphomaniac, and an adulteress. But she does not lose our sympathy because, though promiscuous, she is without vice and grossness. Although animal-like, she gives her heart along with her body; her very excesses spring from a primeval zest for life, and her personality radiates such charm, honesty, and kindliness for all, that she emerges as an eminently lovable creature, a type rare in Maugham. Descriptions of the beauty of heroines of fiction are, as experience shows, usually unconvincing. But, in describing the virginal charm and tranquil beauty of Rosie, Maugham becomes, what is exceedingly unusual for him, passionately lyrical. This emotional exuberance, springing from so unexpected a source, is so strange that it almost succeeds in achieving the impossible.

It is interesting to compare Rosie with Kitty in *The Painted Veil* and with Sophie in a later novel, *The Razor's Edge*. Kitty is too gross and earthy to stand comparison with Rosie. Sophie is another picture of a nymphomaniac, but she does not secure the same sympathy, understanding, and fascination from Maugham as Rosie, and hence remains only a slight sketch.

This is how Rosie's personality may be summed up in Maugham's own words—and the words speak for themselves:

> [She was] all gold, her face and her hair . . . . She glowed, but palely, like the moon rather than the sun, or if it was like the sun, it was like the sun in the white mist of dawn.[13]
>
> She was a very simple woman. Her instincts were healthy and ingenuous. She loved to make people happy. She loved love . . . . It was not vice, it was not lasciviousness; it was her nature. She gave herself as naturally as the sun gives heat or the flowers their perfume. It was a pleasure to her and she liked to give pleasure to others. It had no effect on her character; She remained sincere, unspoiled, and artless.[14]

13 *Ibid.*, 177.
14 *Ibid.*, 249.

Cakes and Ale

Rosie exerts such a powerful fascination over Maugham and monopolizes his sympathy to such an extent that, though there is a hint of pity in the picture of Driffield the man, whose lonely self goes its way under the trappings of a living legend, it only remains a hint. Maugham concerns himself more with the irony of the legend than with the pathos of the lonely soul underneath it. Moreover, just as he makes no attempt to fathom Strickland's mind in *The Moon and Sixpence,* so now, too, he does not try to go deep into Driffield's heart. Here again, however, he makes the same disarming confession of ignorance as in the earlier novel: "I am conscious that in what I have written of him [i.e., Driffield] I have not presented a living man. I have not tried to. I am glad to leave that to the abler pen of Alroy Kear."[15]

The two themes in *Cakes and Ale* are blended perfectly together to make it a marvel of construction. This is all the more remarkable because of the complexity of its structure. This complexity arises out of the fact that the narrative alternately slides backward to the past and forward again to the present, throughout the novel. Thus, the first two chapters set forth the preliminary situation. From the third chapter, the narrative goes back to the past, to the early days of Driffield, until the tenth chapter. In chapter eleven the narrative returns to the present, only to shift backward to the past again until the twenty-first chapter. The next section—chapters twenty-two through twenty-five deals with the present, and the last chapter supplies a missing link in the story. The repeated alternation between the past and the present, however, does not make the story lose either clarity or continuity. This is so because the narrator, Ashenden, can go back conveniently to his memories without giving a jolt to the movement of the story, and Maugham's easy, conversational style does not make the con-

15 *Ibid.,* 247.

tinuous shifting in any way a strain to the reader, while contributing a note of intimacy and verisimilitude to the narrative. Moreover, because the story of the Driffields is told in separate installments, it affords Maugham the opportunity to give us his comments—ironic in the case of Driffield and sympathetic and appreciative in that of Rosie—at the end of each installment.

In *Cakes and Ale*, Maugham, in a sense, returned from the "fresh start" made in *The Moon and Sixpence*. His ironic self is as active and strong as before, but his detachment and aloofness here wilt under the charm of Rosie. The result is very fortunate. For once, both the strains in Maugham gain their complete fulfillment simultaneously and give us his most characteristic work and his most satisfying achievement.

CHAPTER SEVEN

The Last Phase

.

THE TRIUMPH of sensibility in *Cakes and Ale* was an exception, and with his next novel, *The Narrow Corner* (1932), Maugham returned to the ironical aloofness of his middle phase. But the works of this last phase[1] show a development in several new directions. First, there is a distinct realization on the author's part that he is now older and that the world belongs to the young. There is now something almost middle-aged and fatherly in his attitude towards the young. On the other hand, the portraits of those whose race is run gain a certain richness, which is highly significant, and a kind of a farewell-mood prevails in some of the last plays. Secondly, with advancing years comes a greater seriousness, an awareness of the deeper issues of life and a desire to grapple with them, and also a note of introspection. Lastly, age has brought a distinct mellowness.

With the new desire to tackle the deeper issues of life and with the technical mastery which long experience and assiduous practice have brought, Maugham ought to have been able to reach the heights of greatness. The truth appears to be sadly different. Throughout the middle phase, Maugham has sedu-

---

[1] Novels: *The Narrow Corner* (1932); *The Theatre* (1937); *Christmas Holiday* (1939); *Up at the Villa* (1941); *The Razor's Edge* (1944); *Then and Now* (1946); *Catalina* (1948).

Plays: *The Sacred Flame* (1928); *The Breadwinner* (1930); *For Services Rendered* (1932); *Sheppey* (1933).

lously cultivated an ironic aloofness to life and to its major issues, so that it has now become an ingrained habit. It has been indelibly stamped on his very soul. But an ironic acceptance of life, whatever its merits, is woefully inadequate for fathoming the depths of life, which yield their secrets only to insight, feeling, and profound ratiocination. Maugham's ironic indifference has discouraged the free play of these qualities of mind and soul, and now, when he seems to make a demand on himself for them, the demand goes unanswered.

The seven novels of this last phase may be considered under a convenient classification. The seriousness and awareness of the deeper issues of life are most marked in *Christmas Holiday* and *The Razor's Edge*, though there is a distinct, if passing, suggestion of these in *The Narrow Corner*. These three novels may, therefore, be regarded as the major novels of Maugham's last period. Of the remaining four, *Theatre* is a study in passion, but vitiated again, as in *The Painted Veil*, by love being treated as mere animal desire. *Up at the Villa*, too short in range and scope to be considered a novel, is a melodrama, an obvious potboiler. *Then and Now* is a pleasant and rather coarse historical fabliau; while in *Catalina*, Maugham the realist tries his hand at romance for a change, but as is only inevitable, conclusively fails.

The Narrow Corner represents the transition from the middle to the last phase. It possesses substantially both the attitude towards life and the narrative technique of the middle phase. But there is in it, as has already been suggested, a distinct awareness of the greater issues of life. As for its technique and attitude toward life, the whole story is viewed through the eyes of Dr. Saunders, who is a detached and ironic observer of life and who evidently represents here the "I" of the narrator in *The Moon and Sixpence*. Dr. Saunders amusedly watches the drama of love and death and of roguery and self-deception enacted before his eyes in "a narrow corner of the world"—a lonely island in the Pacific, whither accident carries him—but he is himself only a spectator and not an actor in it.

On this tropical isle Dr. Saunders meets Erik Christessen, a romantic idealist and a lover of beauty and knowledge. Erik loves Louise, the daughter of a planter, but his love for her is more of an idealistic dream of his own creation rather than a warm human feeling. Louise, who, it must be said, remains a shadowy figure, falls in love with Fred Blake, a handsome Australian youth, who has come to the island with the doctor. Blake stays only for a couple of days, but this short period is apparently long enough for Louise to yield to temptation. Erik shoots himself, and Fred Blake, filled with remorse, likewise commits suicide, but Louise's comment on the tragedy is, "Don't you think it's rather stupid, the importance men, white men at least, attach to the act of flesh?"[2] Her complaint against Erik is:

> He made a picture of his life and I was to fit in it. He wanted, too, to imprison me in his dream. . . . But I am I. I don't want to dream anybody else's dream. I want to dream my own. All that's happened is terrible and my heart is heavy, but at the back of my mind I know that it's given me freedom.[3]

The theme of *The Narrow Corner* is the tragedy of self-deception. But the novel can hardly be said to rise to the level of true tragedy. One reason for this is that the protagonists of the action are very poorly drawn. Louise, as Pope said of most women, has no character at all. Her fall is not tragic, because there is no struggle whatever in her mind. In fact, she hardly considers herself as fallen, as is evident from her comment on Erik's suicide. Erik Christessen is, on the whole, much better realized than Louise. But he is no tragic hero; for Maugham

2 *The Narrow Corner*, 283.
3 *Ibid.*, 284.

missed a great chance when he passed up the opportunity of giving us a glimpse into the struggle in his hero's heart after the terrible discovery that his ideal is shattered.

The power of tragedy lies in the portrayal of the soul's struggle in the tragic hero. But it is precisely this part of his theme that Maugham hastily skips over as he hurries his hero to his death. Maugham's hands were probably tied by his technique of narration, the serious limitations of which are once again revealed in this case. Dr. Saunders, the ironic spectator, can hardly be expected to understand and appreciate the tragic intensity of a soul's struggle. Fred Blake, the third protagonist of the drama, is hardly a sketch.

The Narrow Corner is, thus, melodrama, not tragedy. That Maugham seems to be more at home with the former than with the latter is substantiated in the long account of the murder committed by Fred Blake in Australia, which is sheer melodrama. Strangely enough, the most vital character in the novel is a minor one—the amusing rascal Captain Nichols, who plays no part in the melodrama proper. He is a scoundrel and a rogue, but he does his "roguing" more for joy than for profit. He is a past master in the art of lying and trickery, but it is impossible to detest him, just as it is impossible to detest Falstaff or Mr. Jingle. Captain Nichols is the first example of how Maugham's irony has become more mellow in this last phase, for, in the diverting account of the funeral where the worthy captain solemnly performs the burial service and in the portrayal of his mortal fear of his wife, there is a touch of pure fun which is rarely to be found in the earlier Maugham.

But the character of Dr. Saunders shows how *The Narrow Corner* has a strong link with the works of Maugham's middle phase. "He was perhaps a cynic,"[4] said Maugham, even though he had earlier illustrated his cynicism fully:

4 *Ibid.*, 128.

Dr. Saunders took an interest in his fellows that was not quite scientific and not quite human. He wanted to receive entertainment from them. He regarded them dispassionately and it gave him the same amusement to unravel the intricacies of the individual as a mathematician might find in the solution of a problem. He made no use of the knowledge he obtained. The satisfaction he got from it was aesthetic and if to know and judge men gave him a subtle sense of superiority he was unconscious of it. . . . The sense of disapproval was left out of him . . . . Right and wrong were no more to him than good weather and bad weather. He took them as they came.[5] . . . He thought it no business of his to praise or condemn. He was able to recognise that one was a saint and another a villain, but his consideration of both was fraught with the same cool detachment.[6] . . . He was much liked. But he had no friends. He was an agreeable companion, but neither sought intimacy nor gave it. There was no one in the world to whom he was not at heart indifferent. He was self-sufficient.[7]

The Captain's philosophy of life is, we are told:

Life is short, nature is hostile, and man is ridiculous.[8] . . . The world consists of me and my thoughts and my feelings; and everything else is mere fancy. There is no possibility and no necessity to postulate anything outside myself.[9]

Dr. Saunders had "long made himself at home in the futility of things,"[10] and he rejoices at the futility because it "gratifies the sense of irony."[11] "He was influenced in his actions neither by love, pity, nor charity,"[12] and if he was sympathetic to his patients, "it was a game that he played, and it gave him

[5] *Ibid.*, 19–20.
[6] *Ibid.*, 72.
[7] *Ibid.*, 20–21.
[8] *Ibid.*, 192.
[9] *Ibid.*, 272.
[10] *Ibid.*, 57.
[11] *Ibid.*, 162.
[12] *Ibid.*, 22.

satisfaction to play it well. . . . He had great natural kindliness, but it was the kindness of instinct, which betokened no interest in the recipient."[13]

This last remark is significant, as it hints at the probable origin of Dr. Saunders' cynicism. Like most cynics, he, too, is a sentimentalist at heart—a sentimentalist, so greatly frightened of sentiment that he consciously develops a cynical "hide" to conceal his emotionality. Fred Blake's summing up of his character in the novel points to the same conclusion: "I thought you were a cynic. You're a sentimentalist."[14]

Dr. Saunders is the most complete picture of a cynic in Maugham's novels. It will easily be seen how Dr. Saunders answers to almost every test of cynicism set forth in chapter I. There is in him the same disposition to look upon life and morals with a frigid indifference, which originates from a conviction that all is vanity, the same absence of warmth, the same distrust of values, which is expressed in irony and sarcasm, the same lack of sympathy, the same feeling of superiority, and, lastly, in him too, cynicism is sentimentalism turning against itself.

Miss Ley, in *Mrs. Craddock*, was an early portrait of a cynic, but it is a mere pencil sketch if compared with the full-scale oil painting of Dr. Saunders. The difference between these two pictures is commensurate with the development of the cynical tendencies in Maugham himself, and, as the story in *The Narrow Corner* unfolds through the narrative of Dr. Saunders, who is the representative of the author, it is possible to see the suggestion of a self-portrait in the person of the cynical doctor.

The note of awareness of the deeper issues of life is faintly apparent, though unmistakably, in *The Narrow Corner*, thus linking it with the novels of Maugham's last phase. This aware-

---

[13] *Ibid.*, 22.
[14] *Ibid.*, 275.

ness is first seen in the portrait of Frith, the planter who is greatly interested in philosophy and, especially, in mysticism. He has ultimately found the solution to the riddle of existence in Brahmanism, which he thinks is "the only religion that a reasonable man can accept without misgiving."[15] Dr. Saunders, too, is interested in the same riddle, though his conclusions are naturally different from those of Frith. Further, the ill luck that dogs Fred Blake, which caused him to leave a trail of blood behind him wherever he went, makes him cry out in anguish, "What does it all mean? Why are we here? Where are we going? What can we do?"—questions in which the young heroes of *Christmas Holiday* and *The Razor's Edge* will also be vitally interested.

Unfortunately, these questions are suggested and tackled in a very perfunctory manner in *The Narrow Corner*, while the gaudy colors of melodrama are laid on with obvious relish. The main charm of the novel lies not in its story, but in its exotic background, which is the fruit of Maugham's fondness for travel, and in some really fine descriptions, including a spirited one of a storm at sea. All this suggests Conrad, but in *Victory* and *Almayer's Folly* the exotic background is the arena of a soul's struggle. In *The Narrow Corner*, it is only a backdrop against which is enacted a rather cheap drama of murder and adultery.

It is significant to note that the final victory in *The Narrow Corner* belongs to cynicism. At the end, having watched the spectacle of self-deception, sorrow, and death, Dr. Saunders complacently concludes that "he was glad he had made the journey. It had taken him out of the rut he had been in so long."[16] It had left him "relaxed as never before from all earthly ties . . . . It was an exquisite pleasure to him to know that there

15 *Ibid.*, 161–62.
16 *Ibid.*, 288.

was no one in the world who was essential to his peace of mind."[17]

In *Christmas Holiday*, the awareness of the serious issues of life is more distinct. The novel relates the story of Charley Mason, a young Englishman brought up in the glass house of a well-to-do middle-class family, who goes to Paris on a holiday during Christmas, determined "to have a lark there." In Paris, he gets more than he has bargained for. He meets life in the raw there and comes face to face with the spectacle of crime and sin, passion and ambition, and misery and remorse. He catches a glimpse of the vast social and political world in Europe through his friend Simon Fenimore, a young journalist, who is a Communist turned Fascist and who wants to do for England what Mussolini and Hitler have done for their respective countries, and also through the Russian refugee prostitute, Lydia, who is the wife of a notorious murderer.

What Charley Mason has seen and heard during his brief stay in Paris enlarges his horizons of thought beyond recognition, and when he returns to England, his life there appears to him to be "nothing but make-believe" and "like a pleasant parlour-game that grown-ups played to amuse children."[18] He feels that "the bottom had fallen out of his world,"[19] for he has looked upon the "Gorgon-face of life," and the experience is unforgettable.

Christmas Holiday was published in 1939, and its background is intended to be that of the troubled years immediately preceding World War II, when the rumblings of the gathering storm were already heard on the horizon. Here was a theme of great sociological and political interest, but here, again Maugham's powers are seen to be inadequate to grapple successfully

17 *Ibid.*, 288.
18 *Christmas Holiday*, 288.
19 *Ibid.*, 289.

90

with it. Thus, the picture of the political horizon is woefully sketchy, consisting, as it does, merely of a few long speeches which Simon is allowed to deliver to his friend from time to time.

To have been made more vivid, the story should have been illustrated, one feels, with a greater variety of scene, situation, character, and human interest. A few journalistic observations can hardly be adequate for the purpose. The intensely realistic picture of the changing social and political scene in *War and Peace* throbs with this kind of pictorial rendering, amplitude, and human warmth. To talk of *Christmas Holiday* in the same breath would almost be committing a sacrilege. The same charge applies to the picture of the Russian refugee, Lydia. This portraiture, too, lacks the amplitude and the depth which could have made it truly tragic.

The uncomfortable thought that Maugham seemed to be more at home in melodrama than in tragedy is once again raised by the fact that what he emphasizes in Lydia is not her tragedy as a refugee, but her afflictions as a murderer's wife. Maugham describes with obvious relish the career of the murderer, Robert Berger—and this, with the account of the crime, takes no less than ninety pages.

Maugham succeeds in two things in *Christmas Holiday*: first, in the ironic picture of the Mason family and their upstart snobbery; and secondly, in the character of Simon Fenimore, another of Maugham's memorable cynics.

The origins of the Mason family go back to the nineteenth century, when Silbert Mason, "who had been head gardener at a grand place in Sussex," married the cook and became a market gardener. From that day the Masons have never looked back. The descendants of Silbert have climbed higher and higher in the social scale, until there is now even a baronet amongst them.

Leslie Mason, Charley's father, is a house agent who has

married an artist's daughter. The Masons are great lovers of culture. They buy the right pictures and admire them, listen to the right music, and read the right books, though they do not like them. They love art so much that they believe that art alone "redeemed human existence from meaninglessness."[20] Yet, when their own son wants to become an artist, they think that the idea is monstrous. But Maugham's irony is mellow and playful here, as in the picture of Captain Nichols in *The Narrow Corner*. One gets the impression that the Masons are snobs— but snobs of so harmless a type that they excite laughter rather than disgust.

Simon Fenimore is the most fully portrayed character in *Christmas Holiday*. He is, even like Miss Ley (*Mrs. Craddock*), Waddington (*The Painted Veil*), and Dr. Saunders, a sentimentalist-turned-cynic. He is described as a tall, thin, young man with restless and suspecting eyes. "His mouth was large and ironical, and he had small irregular teeth that somewhat reminded you of one of the smaller beasts of prey,"[21] and his smile was a sardonic grimace. Simon's being orphaned in childhood warped his personality, but he has no regrets, because, as he puts it, "my mother was a whore, and my father a drunk, I daresay I don't miss much."[22]

Starved of affection and sensitive at heart, Simon is afraid of emotion, which he ruthlessly suppresses. "I can't afford to be soft," he says to his friend, "I can't afford to be tender. When I look into those blue eyes of yours, so friendly, so confiding in human nature, I waver, and I daren't waver. You are my enemy and I hate you."[23] He thinks that art is "nonsense" and love "an instinct that one can't suppress," but which should not be permitted to divert one from one's chosen path. He is self-centered

[20] *Ibid.*, 13.
[21] *Ibid.*, 29.
[22] *Ibid.*, 25.
[23] *Ibid.*, 39.

and self-contented and is certain that within himself are the makings of a world-shaker.

His ambition is to become the right-hand man of a dictator; his idea of a dictator is an individual who must fool all the people all the time, and there's only one way he can do that, he must also fool himself." The dictator has no brains, though he does have "drive, force, magnetism, charm," and hence he must have by his side a strong intellectual who is austere and ruthless and who can rule the people through the dictator. Simon wants to make himself that strong intellectual, and hence his ruthlessness, asceticism, and his contempt for all human values. Simon is evidently not a cynic of the deepest dye, as in his own crazy way he believes in at least certain things. But in him, too, is seen the process of sentimentalism turning sour, which is one chief mark of cynicism. Although Simon is no doubt a fine portrait, one remembers him chiefly as an interesting eccentric.

As for the socio-political background, a glimpse of which is said to have changed Charley Mason's outlook on life, it should have been painted in greater detail by variety of scene and character and with greater realism. But once again, Maugham's habit of playing on the surface, cultivated during the middle phase, and the consequent inability to probe deeper come in the way.

The Razor's Edge is Maugham's most ambitious attempt to pose, and answer, the problem of the meaning of life. The title is taken from the *Katha-Upanishad*: "The sharp edge of a razor is difficult to pass over; thus the wise say the path to salvation is hard." *The Razor's Edge* describes the pilgrimage of the hero, Larry, on to this path. The character of Larry was probably suggested, as William Y. Tindall notes, by the example of Christopher Isherwood, who renounced the world to embrace mysticism.[24] Larry is a zestful, self-possessed, independent-

[24] *Forces in Modern British Literature*, 212.

minded young man, who leads the life of an average American youth until World War II, in which he takes part as an aviator.

Larry's experiences bring about a great change in him. The spectacle of misery and death which he has observed during these years, fills his mind with restlessness and with a longing to find out the answer to the riddle of life. Hence, on coming back, he refuses offers of lucrative positions and decides not to settle down until he has reached his goal.

He explores several avenues in search of Truth. He studies literature and philosophy in a garret in Paris, and when tired of books, he works in a coal mine and on a farm and tramps through Belgium and Germany doing manual work. His quest is still unfinished when he goes to stay in a monastery in Alsace, where he finds Christianity inadequate for his purpose. He then goes to India, where at long last he finds all his questions answered in Hindu mysticism. He stays in an Ashram, meditates, develops Yogic powers, and is granted illumination when out alone in a forest at dawn. "I had a sense," he says while describing the incident, "that a knowledge more than human possessed me so that everything that had been confused was clear and everything that had perplexed me was explained."[25]

Larry's quest is now over. He has found peace, and he returns to America to live "with calmness, forbearance, compassion, selflessness and continence."[26] He decides to renounce his private income and work for his living, earning only as much as will be necessary to provide for his board and lodging, and to devote the rest of his time to what he calls "self-perfection." Larry is, Maugham concludes:

> too modest to set himself up as an example to others; but it may be he thinks that uncertain souls, drawn to him like moths to a candle, will be brought in time to share his own glowing belief

[25] *The Razor's Edge*, 249.
[26] *Ibid.*, 253.

that ultimate satisfaction can only be found in the life of the spirit, and that by himself following with selflessness and renunciation the path of perfection he will serve as well as if he wrote books or addressed multitudes.[27]

Maugham aims very high in *The Razor's Edge*, but there is a great gulf between intention and actual achievement. For here, as John Brophy puts it, "a theme has been chosen which of its own nature makes demands the author is unable to meet."[28] First, the central character is not realized with sufficient power. The novel purports to show the sea change in Larry's mind as he turns from materialistic values to the spiritual. This change cannot come about, in an ordinary man, without severe struggle and trial, without anguish and suffering, or without many a fall crowned ultimately with victory. The actual picture of the change in Larry gives one the impression that the process has been over simplified. Larry has hardly to face any struggle in his progress to salvation, either from enemies within or from without.

"The path to salvation is hard," like "the sharp edge of a razor," says Maugham's motto to the novel. Unfortunately, the sharp edge of the razor is not much in evidence in the novel. Even when Larry has to renounce his love for Isabel, there seems to be no struggle in his heart. He breaks his engagement with her as casually as if he were breaking an appointment of no consequence. His resignation at the very starting point of his progress on to the path of salvation is admirable and saintlike. But, in that case, one feels, he had hardly anything to learn.

Maugham talks about Larry's goodness and disinterestedness, but as John Brophy suggests,

> *The Razor's Edge* . . . seems indeed to invite in the attributed though unrealized character of Larry, a comparison with Dos-

27 *Ibid.*, 283–84.
28 *Somerset Maugham*, 35.

toevsky's *The Idiot*—and the comparison, once begun makes it quite clear that Maugham's place is not among the supreme masters.[29]

Dostoevski's Prince Myshkin is an unforgettable character, for in him is shown the actual process of the purification of the human soul through suffering. The prince is an invalid, whose infirmity makes him renounce all materialistic values and cultivate the Christ-like virtues of charity and kindliness for all. The whole picture has a human warmth and an actuality about it which, by contrast, makes Larry look like a hasty sketch.

Secondly, Maugham's excursions into philosophy in *The Razor's Edge* reveal, even more obviously, the superficiality of the work. His matter-of-fact mind and his love of the concrete probably made it difficult for him to move with ease in the "ampler ether and diviner air" of philosophy. He honestly confessed, in *The Summing Up*, that, though he read "all the most important works of the great classical philosophers . . . with passionate interest" . . . "there is in them a great deal I did not understand, and perhaps I did not even understand as much as I thought";[30] he further adds that Hegel "has consistently bored me."[31] Maugham's accounts of Hindu mysticism and of the ways of the Yogis, as seen through Larry's eyes, is, as might be expected, woefully superficial.

The hypnotism practiced by Larry with the help of the ancient Greek coin after his return from India smacks too much of the "rope trick" variety of spiritualism with which, until lately, Yoga was equated in the average European's mind. On the whole, E. M. Forster's *A Passage to India* shows a keener insight into the Indian mind than *The Razor's Edge*.

Maugham's emotional and spiritual limitations are clearly

[29] *Ibid.*, 35.
[30] *The Summing Up*, 163.
[31] *Ibid.*, 163.

seen in his account of the illumination vouchsafed to Larry. It is the supreme moment of Larry's pilgrimage, yet, as a description of a spiritual experience, it is painfully pedestrian. It does no good to tell the reader, "No words can tell the ecstasy of my bliss."[32] The reader must feel this ecstasy along with the hero, which, one must confess, does not happen here.

It is significant, again, that Maugham's old technique of the detached observer telling the story is, once more, responsible for the lack of depth and power in *The Razor's Edge*. The crucial moments in the story, which are fertile in emotional intensity, are *reported* rather scrappily, and thereby lose much of their power. The account of the death of his friend during the war, which starts Larry on his pilgrimage, and that of the hero's illumination are cases in point.

Of course, from the vantage ground of the detached observer Maugham can disclaim all responsibility for not entering into the innermost recesses of his hero's heart, and this he actually does at the end of the novel. "I am of the earth, earthy," he says, with charming modesty, and "I can only admire the radiance of such a rare creature, I cannot step into his shoes and enter into his inmost heart as I sometimes think I can do with persons more nearly allied to the common run of men."[33] The disarming frankness of his confession may satisfy the ordinary reader (and it certainly has, if one can judge from the number of copies the book has sold), but the discerning reader may murmur ruefully that Maugham has once again fenced with his problem, instead of grappling with it boldly.

Ironically enough, more satisfying than the portrait of Larry is that of the snob, Elliott Templeton, in dealing with whom Maugham is on surer ground. It is a full-length portrait steeped in delicious irony. Elliott is "a colossal snob," the ruling

[32] *The Razor's Edge*, 249.
[33] *Ibid.*, 284.

passion of whose life is "social relationships." He has a passion for hobnobbing with the great and the titled. "He would put up with any affront, he would ignore any rebuff, he would swallow any rudeness to get asked to a party he wanted to go to, or to make a connection with some crusty old dowager of great name."[34] He has his own methods to reach his goal. Thus, when he finds that conversion to Roman Catholicism would open several closed doors to him, he is promptly converted. When at last he is able to invent a noble descent for himself and is made a count by the Pope, he feels that he has reached his Nirvana. For him dressing and attending social parties are almost a ritual to be undertaken devoutly. For him civilization consists of dinner parties.

Nevertheless, the mellowing quality which softened Maugham's irony in his last phase is seen in its purest form in this portrait of Elliott Templeton. He is shown to be kindly, affectionate, considerate and generous to his friends and dear ones. Notwithstanding his affectations, he has a keen sense of beauty and is a discerning judge of art. Maugham feels for the waste of Elliott's life and calls him "the sad Don Quixote of a worthless purpose"; and what is even more significant, he also tries to understand the psychology behind Elliott's snobbery. "At the back of it all," he concludes, "was a passionate romanticism," for in the idle aristocrats with whom he hobnobbed he saw their great ancestors, and thus lived "in a spacious and gallant past."

It is interesting to contrast the portraits of Alroy Kear (*Cakes and Ale*) and Elliott Templeton. In the portrait of Kear, the irony of Maugham is vitriolic throughout the better part of the novel, and when Maugham relents later, Kear only becomes a figure of fun. Maugham is bitter with Kear, but never with Elliott, and at the end, in Elliott's case, Maugham has to offer, not ridicule, but understanding, and even pity.

[34] *Ibid.*, 5–6.

Of the remaining four novels of the last phase, *Theatre*, a
study in passion, tells of the middle-aged actress Julia, on whom
love for the worthless Tom comes as an evil spell which sweeps
her off her feet and releases her only after she has passed through
much suffering and humiliation. Love, in *Theatre*, as in *The
Painted Veil*, is equated with mere animal passion, and like the
earlier novel, *Theatre*, too, cannot escape the taint of coarseness.
The attempt to portray the finer side of passion in Charles
Tamerley, who is said to have loved Julia in vain for twenty
years, is a failure, because in the end it turns out that his love
was the pose of a self-deceiver and not the devotion of a constant lover.

Up at the *Villa*, a book of ninety-two pages, is a long short-
story rather than a novel, centering, as it does, round a single
situation. Mary Panton, a rich young widow, surrenders herself for a single night to a young refugee in a fit of romantic
philanthropy. The youth, upon realizing that he has been the
object of philanthropy and not of love, commits suicide on the
spot. Mary manages to avoid scandal with the help of the
scamp, Rowley Flint, whom she marries. Up at the *Villa* is an
obvious potboiler and a melodrama.

Then and Now is Maugham's second historical novel, the
first being the unsuccessful *The Making of a Saint* (1898). *Then
and Now* succeeds in being interesting, which the earlier novel
did not, but it does little more. Its main theme, which has the
coarse touch of a fabliau about it, rests upon the attempts made
by Niccolo Machiavelli to go to bed with the wife of Bar-
tolomeo, a merchant of Imola—attempts which are frustrated
mainly through Caesare Borgia. The final situation, where
Machiavelli's schemes go awry and the prize for which he has
sweated is snatched away by young Piero, is highly farcical. The
title, *Then and Now*, has a touch of cynicism about it, as if
Maugham wanted to suggest that man is the same sex-

dominated creature, whether in fourteenth-century Italy or in modern England.

The historical background, showing the struggles of Caesare Borgia with his enemies, is strangely confused for so lucid a writer as Maugham; but in Machiavelli himself we have another fine portrait of a cynic. Maugham brings the author of *The Prince* thoroughly to life. His thin lips are "so tightly closed that his mouth was little more than a sarcastic line," and his expression is "wary, thoughtful, severe and cold."[35] Machiavelli is thoroughly unscrupulous and scheming and is an unabashed sensualist. He distrusts all human values. People are merely pawns to be moved about in the fulfillment of his own desires. Here are some of the most significant Machiavellisms in the novel:

> You please [people] more by ministering to their vices than by encouraging their virtues.[36]

> Truth is the most dangerous weapon a man can wield and so he must wield it with caution. For years I have never said what I believed nor even believed what I have said.[37]

> It is good to have friends, but it is as well that they should know you can retaliate if they should be led to act other than as friends should.[38]

> When a woman ceases to be desirable a procuress is born.[39]

> It is not the great deeds men do that make them remembered by posterity, but the fine language with which men of letters describe their deeds.[40]

And lastly, his closing words in the novel:

> In this world if virtue triumphs over vice, it is not because it is virtuous, but because it has better and bigger guns; and if

[35] *Then and Now*, 7.
[36] *Ibid.*, 247.
[37] *Ibid.*, 248.
[38] *Ibid.*, 47.
[39] *Ibid.*, 84.
[40] *Ibid.*, 183.

good overcomes evil, it is not because it is good, but because it has a well-lined purse.[41]

However, it is another proof of Maugham's mellowness in the last phase that he also shows the better side of Machiavelli's character by portraying him as a staunch patriot.

Catalina, Maugham's last novel, is, like his first, the story of a working-class girl. But while *Liza of Lambeth* was starkly realistic, *Catalina* is a romance. It tells of a Spanish girl of the Renaissance who is cured of her lameness by a miracle. She escapes the sainthood which the church wants to thrust upon her and becomes a wife, a mother, and a strolling actress. Maugham's excursion into romance in his last novel is hardly a success. The seven and odd miracles in *Catalina*, including the one when the girl's lameness is cured (one sadly remembers that Philip in *Of Human Bondage* was not so fortunate), though obviously not described with the tongue in cheek, are narrated in a too matter-of-fact style to be impressive, and the historical background is not particularly vivid or alive.

The most significant point about *Catalina* is Maugham's treatment of the clergy. Maugham, the erstwhile scourge of clergymen, is full of understanding and even pity for both Bishop Blasco and Prioress Beatriz. There are, it is true, touches of irony in their portraits, as for instance in the description of the mercy and moderation of the Bishop, who, as inquisitor, burns only seventy people alive and tortures a bare six hundred. Similarly, the quarrel between the Prioress and the Archpriest shows the Roman Catholic Church in one of its less saintly moods.

Irony, however, is not the dominant mood of these portraits. With all his misguided zeal, Bishop Blasco on his death-bed, tortured by remorse, is a pathetic figure. Maugham also shows the aching heart of a woman who had loved in vain

[41] *Ibid.*, 277-78.

beneath the hard, haughty, and domineering exterior of Dona Beatriz, and so important is the revelation in the story that the crucial change in Catalina's fortunes hinges upon it. The wheel has come full circle, for the Maugham of *Liza of Lambeth*, with his understanding and sympathy, seems to return, and a mellowness, which age alone brings, is his now. In *Catalina*, however, Maugham applies these qualities to portraying Bishop Blasco and Prioress Beatriz; the heroine remains a shadowy figure. *Liza*, with its unsparing realism, moves us. But Maugham completely lacks the romantic temper to make the miracle-studded *Catalina* convincing and impressive.

"For some years," says Maugham in the preface to the last volume of his collected plays, "I had in mind the four plays with which I proposed to finish my career as a practising dramatist. I was prepared to write them only on this account, for I did not think any of them was likely to succeed."[42] These four plays are *The Sacred Flame* (1928), *The Breadwinner* (1930), *For Services Rendered* (1932), and *Sheppey* (1933). They, too, show the same features as Maugham's novels of the last phase: the realization that he is no longer young and therefore not "in the movement"; a greater mellowness; and the awareness of the graver issues of life.

The first feature is well substantiated in *The Breadwinner*, which has been described as "an inverted *Doll's House.*" It portrays a middle-aged stockbroker who becomes bored with his job, his routine life, his snobbish wife, and self-centered children, and escapes for his "soul's sake" to travel "in Romance." Maugham's attitude toward the young in the play is significant. He shows them to be completely selfish and self-centered, narrow-minded and intolerant, and hard and brazenly cynical; in short, he views them through the suspecting eyes of one who has left his youth far behind. The cynicism of *The*

[42] *Collected Plays*, Vol. III, p. xvi.

Breadwinner is of a jaded and bored variety. This is what the middle-aged stockbroker thinks about the relationship between parent and child:

> Of course, when they are small, one's fond of one's children. One likes them as one likes puppies or kittens. They're dependent on you, and that's rather flattering. But almost before you know where you are they're young men and women with characters of their own. They are not part of you any more. They are strangers. Why should you care for them?[43]

His wife, who coolly says what a lark it would be if he dies, leaving her free and rich, has no illusions about marriage. "Do you think women find marriage amusing?" she asks, "They have been bored stiff by it for a thousand generations. Half the women I know are so bored by their husbands that they could scream at the sight of them."[44]

And, lastly, this is what the young people in the play think about life: "After all, I did not ask to be brought into the world. He [i.e., father] did it entirely for his own amusement. He must be prepared to pay for it."[45]

For Services Rendered is a ghastly picture of the aftermath of war, ending on a note of savage irony in Eva's hysterical cry, "God save our king." It shows the disillusionment of those of the younger generation who, in Siegfried Sassoon's words, "were destroyed by the War, though they escaped its shells." There is much pity in *For Services Rendered*, but it is the milk of human kindness turned sour. The reason is that there is a total blackout of the positive values in the play. Matthew Arnold rejected his own *Empedocles on Etna*, because he thought that it was not truly tragic since its suffering did not find a "vent in action."

---

[43] *The Breadwinner, Collected Plays*, Vol. III, p. 253.
[44] *Ibid.*, 291.
[45] *Ibid.*, 208.

For Services Rendered fails by the same logic, though it is full of the seriousness of Maugham's last phase.

This note of seriousness is struck in *The Sacred Flame*, also, though here again Maugham missed the authentic tragical note. The play portrays a mother who calmly murders her invalid son, when she finds that the continuance of his life would only bring him dishonor and disillusionment. There is too much of the "detective yarn" in the play, with the secret of the murder being revealed only at the end and with the usual search for a motive and evidence comprising the body of the drama. There is, again, a lack of intensity in the play which prevents it from attaining the tragical level. An undercurrent of philosophy is, no doubt, discernable in some of the speeches of Mrs. Tabret, but, on the whole, there is too much of the "thriller" in the tone of *The Sacred Flame*. Once again, a theme of tragical proportions is handled in a very superficial manner.

The setting of his last play, *Sheppey*, is most unusual for Maugham. The hero is a barber's assistant who, winning an £8,000 prize in the sweepstakes, suddenly decides to spend it all on the poor, which naturally makes his relatives think that the sudden good fortune has unsettled his mind. Maugham says in his preface, "*Sheppey* does not set out to be a problem play; I should describe it as a sardonic comedy."[46] The central situation in the play does, however, suggest a problem in ethics, viz., the conflict between materialism and the claims of the spirit. But considered even as a "sardonic comedy" pure and simple, *Sheppey* does not succeed.

There is no doubt some pungent irony in the scenes where Sheppey's daughter fervently prays to God that her father may be declared mad and when the learned doctor pronounces Sheppey to be a lunatic because, "a sane man is not going to give all his money away to the poor. A sane man takes money

[46] *Collected Plays*, Vol. III, p. xvii.

from the poor." The doctor adds that "philanthropy in general could always be ascribed to repressed homosexuality."[47] Maugham also seems to take a special delight in exposing the snobbery, the self-importance, the cocksureness, and the selfishness of young Florrie and her fiancée, and with cynical glee he further points out how the underdogs, whom Sheppey is so eager to help and reform, ultimately prefer their old crooked ways to receiving charity.

Sheppey, as a whole, however, lacks power: first, because the sudden change in Sheppey in no way appears to be convincing and probable, and thus makes the whole play seem artificial; second, because the sarcasm of the play loses its edge since the struggle between Sheppey and his relatives is not made intense enough. Ibsen's *An Enemy of the People* has virtually the same theme: Dr. Stockmann, too, like Sheppey, goes against the herd and pays the price of his audacity. But Ibsen's play throbs with intense conflict, and the hero has the proper stature to make this conflict powerful. In Ibsen's play the result is tremendous irony, but in Maugham's, the result is pale insignificance. Once again, in *Sheppey*, Maugham has a theme bursting with great potentialities, but they go unrealized.

Sheppey is the last of Maugham's plays. In his preface to Volume VI of the first Collected Edition of his plays (1934), Maugham announced his retirement from the stage, and though critics had prophesied then that it was only temporary, the author kept his word. In the postscript to *A Writer's Notebook* (1949), Maugham wrote that *Catalina* and *Then and Now* were the last of his novels, and that he was "done with fiction also."[48] He remained true to his word. In the preface to the same book Maugham told us, "I have retired from the hurly-burly and ensconced myself not uncomfortably on the shelf I

[47] *Sheppey, Collected Plays*, Vol. III, 285.
[48] Page 287.

have said my say and I am well pleased to let others occupy my small place in the world of letters."[49]

Of the two strains in Maugham, cynicism was the more dominant throughout the middle phase of his work. During this phase, Maugham developed and perfected, as has already been shown, the outlook and the technique of the amused and ironic observer of life, watching his characters and their actions in a detached way from the outside. The disastrous consequences of this outlook and the technique used in dealing with the more serious themes became more conspicuous in the last phase of Maugham's work.

Time and again, in both the novels and the plays of the last period, Maugham sought to grapple with themes that dealt with the eternal riddles of life. But every time he failed to penetrate deep into his subject, failed to warm up sufficiently to it, and failed to instill into it adequate intensity and power.

As for the two strains themselves, Maugham's cynicism was, in this last phase, distinctly tempered by mellowness. But this new mellowness, brought by years, could not, paradoxically enough, produce results similar to those produced by the strong and active sensibility of the early phase, for, it was continually hampered by the confirmed habit of amused indifference cultivated during the middle phase, and was, therefore, not powerful enough to inspire the creative effort required to handle successfully the graver themes at which he now tried his hand.

With regard to form and constructive skill, Maugham the artist is seen to have lost none of his cunning in the last phase. In spite of the limitations of his technique, Maugham remained a skilful artist. This is testified to in *The Razor's Edge*, where the informal style, the changing background, and the building up of the plot through judiciously narrated installments, punctuated with effective breaks, remind one of the artistry of *The*

[49] Pages xii–xiii.

Moon and Sixpence and *Cakes and Ale*. Moreover, with all their shortcomings, these novels are eminently readable. In the plays, too, the way the suspense is sustained throughout *The Sacred Flame* displays the same dramatic skill found in *The Circle*.

Regardless of the virtuosity and readability of Maugham's literary pieces, their lack of penetration and power robbed the author of any positive achievement in the last phase of his career.

CHAPTER EIGHT

The Short Stories

.

I T IS perhaps in his short stories[1] that Maugham's most satisfying achievement is to be found, for his short stories, as a
whole, seem to present a more just and sympathetic picture
of life than is given in most of his plays and novels. Maugham
the cynic is no doubt present in his short stories too. But more
often than not, his amused observation and aloofness are shaken
by the beauty, pathos, and human appeal of his themes, as in
those memorable stories, "Red," "Sanatorium," and "The
Unconquered." To the constructive and technical skill, of
which they have as much as the novels and the plays, there is
added, in many of the stories, a deep emotional warmth. This
is specially to be seen in the stories of the last part of Maugham's
career.

Before tracing the two strains of cynicism and humanitarianism in Maugham's short stories, a brief sketch of his
career as a writer of short stories should be drawn.

It is interesting that Maugham began his literary career as
a writer of short stories, though, as he tells us in the preface to
The Trembling of a Leaf, "I could find no editor to accept
them." Six of these stories form the contents of Maugham's
first volume of short stories, *Orientations* (1899). Maugham

[1] *Orientations* (1899); *The Trembling of a Leaf* (1921); *The Casuarina
Tree* (1926); *Ashenden* (1928); *First Person Singular* (1931); *Ah King* (1933);
Cosmopolitans (1936); *The Mixture as Before* (1940); *Creatures of Circum-
stance* (1947); *The Complete Short Stories*, Three volumes (1951).

seems to have been greatly dissatisfied with these stories, for he did not include any of them in the three volumes of his collected short stories. Between *Orientations* and *The Trembling of a Leaf*, Maugham's next collection of short stories, there is a gap of twenty-two years. The inspiration for this volume came, as Maugham says in the preface, during his journey to the South Seas after World War I. The book won immediate popularity, and since then up to 1947, Maugham published collections of his short stories at regular intervals.

Maugham's career as a writer of short stories may be divided into three phases in the light of the two strains in his work. The first phase, represented by *Orientations*, shows, on the whole, the cynical side of the creator of Liza and Mrs. Craddock. Writing about these stories in the preface to *The Trembling of a Leaf*, Maugham says, "Their worst fault . . . was their superciliousness. In the arrogance of my youth I sneered at everything that offended my fastidious and narrow prejudices."[2]

In half the number of stories in the volume, viz., "Faith," "A Bad Example," and "The Punctiliousness of Don Sebastian," the butt of ridicule is the Roman Catholic Church. The first tells of a Spanish monk who dies as a heretic, but by a strange stroke of irony is canonized. In "The Punctiliousness of Don Sebastian," an archbishop commits adultery. The theme of "A Bad Example" is the tragedy of an ordinary man who tries to put the teaching of Christ into actual practice and is consequently declared insane—a theme to which Maugham returned years later in *Sheppey*. But the native sensibility of the creator of Liza and Bertha Craddock is also seen in some pages of *Orientations*, notably in the long short-story "Daisy," the heroine of which seems to be a first sketch of the lovable Rosie in *Cakes and Ale*.

The stories in *Orientations* are unmistakably crude in tech-

[2] Page xii.

nique and style. In fact, they are anecdotes rather than short stories, and anecdotes told in a stilted style at that. Hence, Maugham has rightly refrained from including any of them in the Collected Edition of his works.

The second phase of Maugham's career as a writer of short stories commences with *The Trembling of a Leaf* (1921), and it may be said to end with *Ah King* (1933). The short stories of these thirteen years were collected in *Altogether* (1934), which thus provides an obvious landmark. This phase roughly coincides with the middle phase of Maugham's work in the fields of fiction and drama. Hence, the characteristic Maugham-manner of the middle phase, consisting of a detached and ironical attitude toward life, dominates the short stories of this phase. But it is significant that in some of the stories written during this period, Maugham's ironical detachment breaks down when his sympathy with some of his creations asserts itself. This, however, happens only in a few cases, and the dominant mood of these stories is one of ironic detachment.

There is ample variety of scene and setting in the stories of this phase. The background for *The Trembling of a Leaf* (1921), *The Casuarina Tree* (1926), and *Ah King* (1933) is Malaya and the South Sea islands. While in *Ashenden* (1928) the setting is mostly Central Europe and the Russia of the Bolshevik Revolution, London provides the scene of most of the stories in *First Person Singular* (1931). But whatever the background, the author's attitude is always that of the amused and ironic observer of life. This attitude may be illustrated from some of the major short stories of this phase. The preface to *Ah King* supports this assertion in its quintessence. The book was named after Ah King, the Chinese servant who accompanied the author on his journey through the East. When, at the end of the journey, the time to part came, Ah King was in tears. Maugham's reaction to this makes significant reading:

It had never occurred to me for an instant that he looked upon me as anything but an odd, rather silly person who paid his wages. . . . That he had any feeling for me never entered my head. I was embarrassed. . . . It is for these tears that I now give his name to this collection of stories.[3]

As R. A. Cordell rightly remarks, "perhaps Maugham's incomprehension in this case is significant; there may be more simple, unselfish affection in heaven and earth than is dreamt of in his philosophy."[4]

Maugham began his career as a successful short-story writer with "Rain" (*The Trembling of a Leaf*), which followed the juvenile *Orientations*. This collection sets the pattern of the characteristic Maugham-manner. "Rain," one of the most popular of Maugham's tales, portrays the conflict between the spiritual and the sensual. It tells of a missionary—Maugham's favorite butt of ridicule—filled with fanatic religious zeal, who attempts to reform a vulgar prostitute. By a savage stroke of irony, it is the prostitute who wins in the struggle, by making the missionary fall prey to temptation. He kills himself, and the story ends with the prostitute's cryptic comment, which comes like a whiplash: "You men! You filthy, dirty pigs! You're all the same, all of you pigs! Pigs!"

The struggle is viewed through the eyes of Dr. Macphail, who represents the usual detached observer in the Maugham-manner. Our sympathies are enlisted neither for the missionary who falls nor for the prostitute who is persecuted by him. She remains a vulgar and odious woman, and the picture of the missionary and his wife is full of biting irony. Thus, we have the missionary's chief complaint against the natives of the South Sea island where he works.

When we went there they had no sense of sin at all. They broke

[3] *Ah King*, iii–iv.
[4] R. A. Cordell, *W. Somerset Maugham*, 275.

the Commandments one after the other and never knew that they were doing wrong. And I think that was the most difficult part of my work, to instil into the natives the sense of sin.[5]

The missionary's wife is a prig. She wants to describe the "shocking marriage customs" of the natives to Dr. Macphail, but her sense of delicacy does not allow her to do so. So the way out is, "I'll tell Mrs. Macphail and she'll tell you"; when the process is complete, the missionary's wife cries exultantly, "Well, what did I say to you? Did you ever hear anything more dreadful? You don't wonder that I couldn't tell you myself, do you?"[6]

"Rain" is outwardly, a highly impressive story on account of its theme, which is rich in conflict, its dramatic ending, and its highly effective background of rain. But the reader's inability to sympathize with any single character in the story detracts much from its aesthetic appeal.

The ironical detachment in "Rain" grows into a cynical negation of values in "The Back of Beyond" (*Ah King*) and "Virtue" (*First Person Singular*). The theme of both is that virtue is a fig. "Honour be damned. One has one's happiness to think of. Is one's honour really concerned because one's wife hops into bed with another man?"[7] asks George Moon, the detached observer who evidently represents the author in the story "The Back of Beyond." Hence, Moon advises his friend, whose wife has been unfaithful to him, to forgive her, not out of generosity and large heartedness, but simply because the whole thing is much ado about nothing.

In "Virtue," the middle-aged, married Margery falls in love with young Morton, but being a virtuous woman, refuses to have an affair with him. She merely leaves her uxorious husband, who commits suicide. Of the tragedy the narrator comments:

[5] *The Complete Short Stories*, Vol. I, 10.
[6] *Ibid.*, Vol. I, 3.   [7] *Ibid.*, Vol. III, 1184.

It's her goodness that has caused all the trouble. Why on earth didn't she have an affair with Morton? Charlie would have known nothing about it and wouldn't have been a penny the worse. She and Morton could have had a grand time and when he went away they could have parted with the consciousness that a pleasant episode had come to a graceful end. It would have been a jolly recollection, and she could have gone back to Charlie satisfied and rested and continued to make him the excellent wife she had always been. . . . Virtue be damned. A virtue that only causes havoc and unhappiness is worth nothing. You call it virtue if you like. I call it cowardice.[8]

In both the stories, the narrator, accused of cynicism, defends himself as follows:

If to look truth in the face and not resent it when it is unpalatable, and take human nature as you find it, smiling when it is absurd and grieved without exaggeration when it is pitiful is to be cynical, then I suppose I am a cynic. Mostly human nature is both absurd and pitful, but if life has taught you tolerance you find in it more to smile at than to weep.[9]

In another short story he says that "If it's cynical to look truth in the face and exercise commonsense in the affairs of life, then certainly I am a cynic."[10] This spirited defense is not, however, completely successful, for the narrator forgets that "to look truth in the face" need not mean the denial of all values, and that his so-called tolerance is suspiciously like the frigid indifference of the cynic which, as has been shown earlier, originates out of the conviction that " all is vanity."

This attitude is indicated by the ending of "The Back of Beyond," where the narrator, reflecting on human nature, remembers the absurd and meaningless movements of the small

[8] *Ibid.*, Vol. II, 631.
[9] "The Back of Beyond," *The Complete Short Stories*, Vol. III, 1167.
[10] "Virtue," *The Complete Short Stories*, Vol. II, 631.

fish which he has often observed "in the dry creeks of certain places along the coast." His final comment is significant: "They [the fish] reminded you very much of human beings. It was quite entertaining to stand there for half an hour and observe their gambols."[11]

An incident in "The Human Element" (*First Person Singular*) reveals Maugham's dread of sentiment and his eagerness to suppress it, which are, among others, the characteristic features of his middle phase. A casual acquaintance of the narrator says suddenly to him, "I'm so desperately unhappy." The narrator's reaction is characteristic of Maugham.

> He said it without warning. I cannot describe what a shock it was to me to hear him say these words. I felt as you do when you turn a corner of the street and on a sudden a great blast of wind meets you, takes your breath away, and nearly blows you off your feet. . . . After all I hardly knew the fellow. . . . It was amazing that a man so self-controlled, so urbane, accustomed to the usages of polite society, should break in upon a stranger with such a confession. I am naturally reticent. I should be ashamed, whatever I was suffering, to disclose my pain to another. I shivered. His weakness outraged me. How dared he thrust the anguish of his soul on me? I very nearly cried, "What the hell do I care?"[12]

In *Ashenden*, we find an elaborate picture of the cynical propensities in Maugham. As John Brophy points out, Ashenden's "first name is the same as Maugham's, the background of his youth resembles Maugham's and he, as Maugham tells us in the introduction to the film *Trio*, may be taken as a 'flattering' self-portrait."[13] Maugham tells us:

Ashenden admired goodness, but was not outraged by wicked-

11 *The Complete Short Stories*, Vol. III, 1187.
12 *The Complete Short Stories*, Vol. II, 997–98.
13 *Somerset Maugham*, 28.

ness. People sometimes thought him heartless because he was more often interested in others than attached to them and even in the few to whom he was attached his eyes saw with equal clearness the merits and the defects. When he liked people it was not because he was blind to their faults, he did not mind their faults but accepted them with a tolerant shrug of the shoulders, or because he ascribed to them excellences that they did not possess.[14]

Ashenden is, like Maugham, a detached observer of life. People, "his raw material, did not bore him any more than fossils bore the geologist."[15] He has, we are told, "a confident belief in the stupidity of the human animal."[16] Ashenden's philosophy of human nature makes interesting reading. He believes:

Vanity is the most . . . universal and the most ineradicable of the passions that afflict the soul of man, and it is only vanity that makes him deny its power. . . . It is part and parcel of every virtue. . . . It leers even cynically in the humility of the saint.[17]

The supreme importance ascribed to vanity in Ashenden's philosophy has a close parallel in that prince of cynics, Rochefoucauld.

The stories in *Ashenden,* accordingly, show a lack of warmth due to mere objective observation involving the repression of the author's sympathies, in spite of the fact that they are eminently readable. The point is well illustrated by two of the stories, "His Excellency" and "Giulia Lazzari." The former is an almost complete repetition of the Mildred-Philip episode in *Of Human Bondage.* But in the novel our sympathies are enlisted for the lonely adolescent Philip. Here the victim is only a weak-kneed youth, whose infatuation merely arouses a faint

14 *Ashenden,* 178.
15 *Ibid.,* 100.
16 *Ibid.,* 14–15.
17 *Ibid.,* 230–31.

disgust. In "Giulia Lazzari," too, the love story of the Indian revolutionary and the Italian dancer fails to attain the level of tragedy for the author's sympathies are ruthlessly supressed.

In only a single story in the book does Maugham's detachment break down, and this story, "Mr. Harrington's Washing," has, as will be shown later, a rich human warmth.

As has been pointed out earlier, not all the stories of this phase show cynicism to be the dominant strain. In some of them we have crisp but playful irony in place of cynicism, and in others both cynicism and irony are engulfed in an upsurge of sympathy. Choice examples of either type may be given. "Jane," "The Round Dozen," and "The Creative Impulse" (all from *First Person Singular*) are all redolent of good-humored irony. In "Jane" the humor arises out of surprise, when a commonplace middle-aged woman is suddenly rejuvenated, to become a society belle of charm and wit, much to the chagrin of her sister-in-law. Humor and irony join hands in "The Round Dozen," where the picture of Mortimer Ellis who marries a dozen women has a touch of farce about it, and that of the snobbery of the St. Clair family is full of gentle irony.

"The Creative Impulse" is a satire on high-brow authors, but it is not bitter as are the early pages of *Cakes and Ale*. The snobbish Mrs. Forrester is a high-brow poetess. Her major title to literary fame is, we are told, that she had discovered "the comic possibilities of the semi-colon." She is the tin goddess of her coterie, in which a subject for serious discussion on one occasion was whether the great poetess should shingle her hair or not. There is exquisite fun when the bored husband of the poetess elopes with her cook. When the crestfallen poetess goes to persuade her erring husband to return, the cook tells her, "I've left all my menus with the new cook ma'am," which well-meant but matter-of-fact remark makes it impossible for the poetess to bring her emotion into play, with the result that she comes back alone and decides to inflict her vengeance on the world by writing a detective story. Maugham's irony is here playful and his laughter free and genial.

But the most appealing stories of the second phase are those in which Maugham's sympathy breaks through the cover of ironic detachment, though their number is very small. The best of these is the story "Red" (*The Trembling of a Leaf*) which, significantly enough, Maugham selects as his best story.[18] Its theme is universal. It has been expressed with classical perfection in Keats's lines:

> . . . *Beauty cannot keep her lustrous eyes*
> *Or new Love pine at them beyond to-morrow.*

"Red" is suffused with deep pity for young love and beauty which heed not Man's Faustus-like cry, "Stay, thou art so fair," but hasten to decay. It is an exquisite prose idyll of the love of a young couple on a lonely green island in the Pacific. Maugham's usually pedestrian style glows with warmth and color in describing the place.

And presently I found out why the spot had such an unearthly loveliness. Here love had tarried for a moment like a migrant bird that happens on a ship in mid-ocean and for a little while folds its tired wings. The fragrance of a beautiful passion hovered over it like the fragrance of hawthorn in May in the meadows of my home.[19]

Here young and handsome Red and Sally live and love. It is not death that parts them. It is Time "with a gift of tears" that kills their love. For "the tragedy of love is not death or separation. . . . The tragedy of love is indifference."[20]

The tragedy is viewed through the eyes of Neilson, who

[18] Maugham selected "Red" as his best short story for inclusion in "My Best Story": *An Anthology of Stories by their own authors* (1929).
[19] *The Complete Short Stories*, Vol. III, 1520.
[20] *Ibid.*, 1531.

tries to be the detached observer of the Maugham-manner, but does not succeed since his sympathies cannot be repressed. Describing Neilson, Maugham says, "It was as though he spoke from emotion which his intellect found ridiculous. He had said himself that he was a sentimentalist, and when sentimentality is joined with scepticism there is often the devil to pay."[21] Fortunately, sentiment wins over detachment in "Red," and the result is an unforgettable story rich in human warmth. Red and Sally are the eternal lovers—symbols of love and beauty. The universality of its theme, its rich compassion, and its poetic descriptions make "Red" one of the most appealing of Maugham's short stories.

Maugham's compassion is again in evidence in "The Pool" (*The Trembling of a Leaf*) and "The Force of Circumstances" (*The Casuarina Tree*), both of which have the same theme— the tragedy of the disastrous union of the European with a native woman. The mingling of the two cultures makes only for disharmony. The tragedy in the former story is more powerful, because it is enacted against the background of the pool, which becomes a symbol of the beauty of the East—beauty which is only a *Belle Dame sans Merci* for the European.

"The Alien Corn" (*First Person Singular*) is a touching study of the attempts of two rich Jewish parents, who have been naturalized as English, to make an English gentleman of their son. The alien sapling cannot take root in the foreign soil and withers away. The tragedy of the son is told with sincere compassion which outweighs the irony in the portrait of the parents.

For once, even in the *Ashenden* stories, Maugham forgets his ironical detachment and pauses to admire affectionately Mr. Harrington in "A Chance Acquaintance." Mr. Harrington is a snob and a bore, a type on which Maugham's acid irony thrives.

[21] *Ibid.,* 1520.

But here his irony becomes gentler, because he is able to see what is lovable in the snob and the bore. Mr. Harrington is an impossible companion, an exasperating busybody, and a ridiculous prig. But he is kind and generous and heroic in death. Ashenden's conclusion, "Mr. Harrington was absurd, but lovable,"[22] is an admission of defeat on the part of the amused and detached observer of human nature.

But the occasions on which Maugham's detachment wilts under the pressure of compassion are few, and the dominant mood of the stories of the middle phase remains that of amused detachment, which, as has been shown earlier, frequently shades off into cynical indifference. The result is, though these stories are readable and well told, one is, on the whole, painfully conscious of a certain lack of warmth in most of them.

The final phase of Maugham's career as a writer of short stories may be said to comprise his last three collections of short stories: *Cosmopolitans* (1936), *The Mixture As Before* (1940), and *Creatures of Circumstance* (1947). This phase coincides roughly with the last phase of Maugham's career as a writer of fiction and presents almost similar features. Maugham's acid irony has softened down here, as there, into good-humored banter; there is a distinct mellowness in his outlook on human nature, with a desire to understand and condone the little frailties of men.

This change is unmistakably seen in *Cosmopolitans*. In the story "Salvatore," Maugham attempts something which he has very rarely tried to do so far. The story which opens with the words "I wonder if I can do it" goes on to sketch the life of a poor fisherman, a simple kindly soul, who with his native wisdom practices resignation in a way which saints might envy. At the conclusion of the story Maugham explains what he has tried to do in the tale.

22 *Ashenden*, 266.

W. Somerset Maugham

I wanted to see whether I could hold your attention for a few pages while I drew for you the portrait of a man, just an ordinary fisherman who possessed nothing in the world except a quality which is the rarest, the most precious and the loveliest that anyone can have. Heaven only knows why he should so strangely and unexpectedly have possessed it. And in case you have not guessed what the quality was, I will tell you. Goodness, just goodness.[23]

Thus, the chronicler of marital inconstancy and the detached observer suspicious of all motives has now come to perceive goodness, "just goodness."

The prevailing mood of these stories is neither one of cynical detachment nor of acid irony. Time and again in this phase, Maugham, full of understanding for the creatures of his imagination, admires and appreciates, pities and is moved. And when he laughs at frailty, it is not the withering grimace of the misanthrope that we see, but the genial smile of Puck. Thus, in "Louise" (*Cosmopolitans*) Maugham laughs at a self-indulgent woman who makes capital use of the weak heart which she is supposed to have, to get what she wants. She outlives her two husbands, and when her daughter, who has come of age, wants to go to a party, Louise immediately has one of her heart attacks. Her daughter at last decides to marry, and Louise has her last heart attack on the wedding day. There is a touch of exaggeration in the story which makes its tone humorous rather than ironical.

The same humorous exaggeration marks "The Facts of Life" (*The Mixture as Before*), "The Wash-Tub" (*Cosmopolitans*), and "The Three Fat Women of Antibes" (*The Mixture as Before*). In the first story, a young man who goes to Monte Carlo for the first time is warned by his worldly-wise father against three things—gambling, lending money, and

[23] *The Complete Short Stories*, Vol. III, 1297.

women. The young man meddles with all these three and, by a stroke of irony, instead of burning his fingers, is the richer for it, leaving his father crestfallen. "The Wash-Tub" tells of an American lady who captivates London society by representing her husband who is a prosaic professor as a wild "Western" hero, with the result that the poor husband has to continue to disappear for fear of being exposed. Farce dominates "The Three Fat Women," which is a comedy of middle-aged corpulence ending in a sea of butter and toast.

Another fine example of the new mellowness which Maugham's irony has acquired in the last phase is provided by "Winter Cruise" (*Creatures of Circumstance*). Miss Reid, the main character in the story, is a great bore. The only passenger on board a German ship, she bores the crew so much with her incessant questions that they decide to take vengeance on her on New Year's Eve. They persuade the young radio operator to make love to her, which suddenly makes her aloof and silent. She is now so kind to the crew that they hate themselves for their duplicity and weep when their passenger leaves them. Neither the crew nor Miss Reid loses our sympathy, and we laugh at the irony of circumstances.

Maugham's irony does not only become mellow in these stories, but it frequently gives place to pure humor, as in the stories, "Luncheon" and "Raw Material." In the former, the impecunious narrator invites a lady to luncheon. The lady orders all expensive dishes of food, much to the chagrin of the poor host. He has his revenge, however, when some years later he again meets the glutton, who now weighs twenty-one stone! In the latter story, the narrator mistakes two respectable Americans for cardsharps and reconstructs their characters with his imagination, only to realize the truth in the end.

The best stories of the last phase are those in which the author gives free rein to his sense of compassion, and their number is larger here than in the middle phase. "Sanatorium" is a deeply moving portrayal of the power of love. In a nursing home for consumptive patients, love springs up between Templeton, who has only a few more years to live, and Ivy Bishop. The lovers are warned by the doctor that, if they marry, Templeton will die within six months. The lovers prefer love and death to safety. Their heroic decision electrifies the sanatorium.

> Even the dullest were moved at the thought of these two persons who loved one another so much that they were prepared to sacrifice their lives. A spirit of kindliness and good will descended on the sanatorium. People who hadn't been speaking spoke to one another again . . . . The great love that had taken possession of the man and the girl seemed to spread its effulgence on all that came near them.[24]

The end is touching. Henry Chester, one of the patients, who has been so greatly frightened of death that he has begun to hate the sight of his wife who looks so healthy, is now reconciled to the thought of death and speaks to his wife about it.

> All this about Templeton and Ivy Bishop—I don't know how to put it, it's made me see everything differently. I don't mind dying any more. I don't think death's very important, not so important as love. And I want you to live and be happy. I don't grudge you anything any more and I don't resent anything. I'm glad now it's me that must die and not you. I wish for you everything that's good in the world. I love you.[25]

The events in the story are viewed through the eyes of Ashenden, who himself is a patient in the sanatorium. But he is a different Ashenden from the one in the ironical *Ashenden* stories of the middle phase. Maugham attempts a defense of Ashenden here as there. "People often said he [Ashenden] had

[24] *The Complete Short Stories*, Vol. II, 928–29.
[25] *Ibid.*, 930.

a low opinion of human nature. It was because he did not always judge his fellows by the usual standards. He accepted, with a smile a tear or a shrug of the shoulders, much that filled others with dismay."[26] But Ashenden here does not merely accept things as they are. He admires, appreciates and is moved, and is no longer the ironic observer of the middle phase. Maugham's glorification of love here is in perfect contrast with the "sexiness" of *The Painted Veil* and *Theatre*, where love is mere animal passion; the tenderness with which the lovers are treated and Henry Chester's change of heart as shown is rarely to be found in the Maugham of the middle phase.

In "Gigolo and Gigolette" (*The Mixture as Before*) is painted the hard lot of Stella the "stunt queen." She risks her life twice every day for the fickle public who turn up again and again for the performance in the ghoulish hope that one day she might be killed. She realizes the futility of it all when one day she meets an old painted woman who has been in her time a great stunt queen as famous "as The Tower of London" but is now only a ridiculous nonentity. But Stella cannot abandon her profession though she hates it, as that would mean starvation. She must go through her nerve-shattering ordeal twice a day. "I mustn't disappoint my public," she concludes. The theme of the story has a strong resemblance to that of Maupassant's "Julie Romain," which presents a famous actress, neglected and lonely in her old age, but still clinging pathetically to her lost youth and glory. In both the stories there is a curious blend of irony and sympathy, and in both, sympathy wins in the end.

The "Lotus Eater" (*The Mixture as Before*) is the tragedy of a man who decides to give himself twenty-five years of leisure, comfort, and happiness at a health resort, after which his plan is to call it a day and end his life. Twenty-five years pass, but pro-

[26] *Ibid.*, 917.

longed happiness has snapped all strength of character in this lotus-eater. He does not have the courage to end his life; he drifts and dies a total wreck. The degeneration in his character is portrayed without irony, rather with deep pity for the weakness of human nature.

"The Mother" (*Creatures of Circumstance*) is a study in abnormal psychology. La Cachirra, the mother, is a repulsive hag, a quarrelsome, mean, miserly woman with an impossible temper. Yet there is something almost heroic in her fierce love for her son, for whose sake she kills her own lover. The story has a powerful ending—she kills the young girl who has dared to come between the lioness and her whelp. La Cachirra is a criminal, yet she is not detestable. There is something almost awe-inspiring in her ferocious mother passion.

Perhaps the most powerful of Maugham's stories is "The Unconquered" (*Creatures of Circumstance*), for here, the detached and ironic observer of the Maugham-manner is absent and the emotional possibilities of the theme are fully exploited. The scene is wartime France under German occupation. Hans, a German soldier, under the influence of drink, rapes a French farmer's daughter, Annette. Later, when he comes to know that she is with child, a great wave of love surges up in his heart for the mother of his child. He decides to make her a reparation by marrying her. Her parents, whose animosity breaks down under his helpful ways, give their consent. But Annette, refusing to be reconciled, has her revenge, and a terrible revenge it is. She drowns her child with her own hands in the stream as soon as it is born. The story ends in this manner:

> Hans gave a great cry, the cry of an animal wounded to death; he covered his face with his hands, and staggering like a drunken man flung out of the door. Annette sank into a chair, and leaning her forehead on her two fists burst into passionate weeping.[27]

[27] *The Complete Short Stories*, Vol. I, 308.

The story is told in the third person, and the detached on-looker in the normal Maugham-story does not interfere with the action here. The story derives its power from the intense struggle between Hans and Annette. This struggle illustrates Hegel's dictum that tragedy is a clash between two forces both of which are just. Hans is no villain. His repentance, his desire to make a reparation to his victim, and his grief at the murder of his son are all genuine. He claims our sympathy in the end, but so does Annette, whose murder of her child is a gesture at once horrible, pathetic, and heroic. Moreover, there are rich over-tones of universality in the story, for the tragedy of Annette is the tragedy of countless women since Medea. Above all, Maugham does not flinch from emotion in "The Uncon-quered." Restraint is no doubt exercised in the telling of the story, but the deep pity behind it is unmistakable.

Thus, in the last phase of Maugham's career as a writer of short stories, sympathy wins all along the line and gives to these stories a rich humanity which is but occasionally present in the stories of the two earlier phases. One therefore feels like return-ing to *Cosmopolitans, The Mixture as Before,* and *Creatures of Circumstance,* which can hardly be said about many stories from the earlier phases. In fact, in contrast with the last novels, in these stories of the last phase the new mellowness is very rarely hampered by the habit of amused indifference, because Maugham's sympathy has on the whole received freer scope in his short stories.

The strains of cynicism and humanitarianism are present in Maugham's short stories also. But, on the whole, his short stories seem to present a fairer, more balanced, and a more humane picture of life and human nature than his novels and his dramas taken as a whole do. Perhaps this is so because Maugham, writing his short stories in the intervals of producing his novels and plays, was unconsciously taking a holiday from his cynical detachment. Cynicism and ironic detachment no doubt mark many of the stories, but the number of occasions on which the writer's emotion and sympathy are given free play are more frequent here than in the novels and the plays. It is possible, therefore, that posterity might find Maugham's short stories more appealing than his other works.

Maugham's technique as a writer of short stories will be considered later, however, some of his salient excellences and limitations as a short-story writer will be indicated here. Maugham's limitations in the short stories, as in the novels and the plays, are many. There is in them an almost total lack of poetry, as in his novels and plays. Hence his descriptions of the East, though adequate for the purposes of the stories, hardly bring out the magic of the Orient as Conrad, for example, frequently does. Thus, in Conrad's "Typhoon," as A. C. Ward[28] points out, the reader actually feels "the clammy heat which made the air seem thick, and made Captain MacWhirr gasp like a fish." Maugham's description of the rain in "Rain" is no doubt more than adequate for the purpose of setting the story against an appropriate and effective background, but as an exercise in description it can hardly match the sensuous appeal of the background of Conrad's story.

Similarly, romance is totally out of Maugham's ken. Thus, when he tries his hand at the supernatural in a story like "Lord Mountdrago" (*The Mixture as Before*), he fails as decisively as Kipling succeeds in creating an uncanny effect in a story like *The Mark of the Beast*. Then again, Maugham's completely objective and frequently detached method results, in weak moments, in mere reportage, as in stories like "The Book Bag" (*Ah King*) and "The Kite" (*Creatures of Circumstance*), where the bare recording of the actions of the characters, without any attempt at understanding and explaining the motives

[28] *Aspects of the Modern Short Story*, 123.

behind them, leaves the reader dissatisfied and creates an impression of cheapness and superficiality.

Moreover, as already noted, the stories in which cynicism dominates leave an unpleasant taste in the mouth, which has prejudiced many people against Maugham's stories in general. "There is evidently something that a number of people do not like in my stories,"[29] admits Maugham in the preface to *Altogether*, and this "something" seems to be the lack of warmth which characterizes some of them.

Lastly, Maugham's style, specially in the stories, is hopelessly riddled with clichés which trip over one another throughout each of his tales. The list of the things which Maugham could not do in the field of the short story is a long one.

However, Maugham's excellences as a short-story writer are many and various. No other English short-story writer is as completely a citizen of the world as he is. There is God's plenty in the variety of scene and setting in his stories. And what a rich display of the many-sidedness of human character do those tales show! Maugham has a quick eye for human frailty, here as in his other works, but here he frequently admires, appreciates, understands, and pities. His sense of dramatic situation and of perfect construction and flawless form is also worthy of admiration. Suffice it to say here, these qualities are among some of the major excellences of his works. When all these are combined with deep sympathy and sincere emotion, we have such appealing and powerful stories as "Red," "Sanatorium," and "The Unconquered."

Maugham makes no attempt to strike out on new paths in the field of short-story technique, no attempt at formal or stylistic innovations, like James, Joyce, or William Saroyan. He has founded no school, nor has his influence been wide. All this, together with the fact that his cynical and ironical stories

[29] Page xxv.

are perhaps better known than those in which his sympathy receives free play, has created the fashion to look down upon his short stories. But nowhere else is Maugham's claim to the title "the English Maupassant" more justified than in his short stories; Maugham's short stories, specially those of his last phase, do show all the qualities—the mixture of irony and deep sympathy, the unerring eye for character, the restraint and the objectivity, and the sense of flawless form—and limitations that are characteristic of Maupassant's work. It is significant that Maugham's short stories have been "better appreciated in France than in England."[30]

[30] *The Summing Up*, 143.

CHAPTER NINE

The Travel Books

·

IN HIS AUTOBIOGRAPHICAL *Summing Up*, Maugham described
himself as having been "more of a traveller than most
writers."[1] The claim was not an empty boast for Maugham was
one of the most widely traveled modern English writers. Malaya,
the South Sea Islands, China, Burma, India, Spain, and Russia
—the list of trophies in the bag of Maugham the traveler is a
long one. It is, therefore, surprising to discover that his prolific
literary output includes less than half a dozen travel books.
These are *The Land of the Blessed Virgin* (1905), *On a Chinese
Screen* (1922), *The Gentleman in the Parlour* (1930), and *Don
Fernando* (1935, revised ed. 1950). Apart from these, A
Writer's Notebook (1949) includes several notes made by
Maugham during the course of his travels.

   *The Land of the Blessed Virgin—Sketches and Impres-
sions of Andalusia,* Maugham's first travel book, was written
when, at the age of twenty-three, he went to Seville. The story
of the genesis of the book is told in *Don Fernando*[2] and *The
Summing Up.*[3] Maugham took a trip on horseback through
Andalusia and wrote an account of the excursion. He had at that
time been playing the sedulous ape to Walter Pater and Jeremy
Taylor, and he wrote this account "as an exercise in style." He

---

[1] *The Summing Up,* 99.
[2] Pages 50–51.
[3] Page 26.

added to it descriptions of Seville and other places in Andalusia. Maugham, who is perhaps the most severe critic of his own work, calls the book "crude and gushing."[4] Regarding its style, Maugham observes, "It has neither ease nor spontaneity. It smells of hot-house plants."[5] With his characteristic irony Maugham speaks about the nature of the descriptions in the book:

> It is curious how seldom youth looks at the world with the fresh and direct gaze that you would have expected to come naturally to him; whether from diffidence or timidity, he looks upon what he has never seen before with alien eyes. Perhaps a certain sophistication is needed before one can see things for oneself. Such certainly was the case with me. My feelings were genuine enough, but they were the feelings of the travellers who had gone before me. I saw what Borrow and Richard Ford, Théophile Gautier and Mérimée had seen.[6]

Yet, in spite of its obvious immaturity, *The Land of the Blessed Virgin* does suggest the promise that Maugham's mature travel books were to fulfill. His keen power of observation is already in evidence in passages like the description of the grotesque ugliness of old Spanish women; his barbed irony is already at work—though it is not ubiquitous yet—as in his comment on the self-righteous attitude of the English towards bull-fighting; his eye for human character and its oddities is revealed in his analysis of the Spanish habit of lying. It is only when Maugham labors at the purple patch—and that he does distressingly often here—as in his attempt to paint a terrible and sinister picture of the landscape after Browning's *Childe Roland*, that we realize fully the immaturity of the book.

Seventeen years after *The Land of the Blessed Virgin* fol-

[4] *Don Fernando*, 51.
[5] *The Summing Up*, 26.
[6] *Don Fernando*, 50.

lowed *On a Chinese Screen.* "This is not a book at all," declares
Maugham in his preface, "but the material for a book."[7] During his journey through China in 1920, Maugham made "notes
of the people and places" that excited his interest. His plan was
to gather material for novels and stories. As the notes grew
voluminous, Maugham decided to make them into a connected
narrative of the journey. During the seventeen years that
separate *On a Chinese Screen* from the earlier travel book,
Maugham had already made a name as a brilliant exponent of
the comedy of manners and had already emerged, in *The Moon
and Sixpence,* as an ironic observer of life. The chief excellence
of *On a Chinese Screen,* therefore, lies in the incisively drawn
portraits both of the Chinese and of the Europeans in China.

Regarding *The Gentleman in the Parlour,* Maugham
tells us:

> This book is not like *On a Chinese Screen,* the result of an acci-
> dent. I took the journey it describes because I wanted to; but I
> had from the beginning the intention of writing a book about
> it. I had enjoyed writing *On a Chinese Screen.* I wanted to try
> my hand again on the same sort of subject, but on a more
> elaborate scale and in a form on which I could impose a definite
> pattern. It was an exercise in style.[8]

The Gentleman in the Parlour, which is a record of a journey
from Rangoon to Haiphong, is thus a more ambitious book
than its predecessor. It gives us, along with sketches of the
Oriental and European types, passages of set description, criticism of art and architecture, and the author's reflections on
life and the world.

In *Don Fernando,* the last of Maugham's travel books, the
wheel comes full circle. He returns to the subject of his first
travel book, Spain. But in *Don Fernando,* Maugham travels

[7] *Ibid.,* ix.
[8] Page vii.

through time as well as through space. For, the Spain of *Don Fernando* is the Spain of the Golden Age, not that of the twentieth century. Here again, Maugham tells us that his original intention was not to write a travel book at all. "These essays on various aspects of Spanish life during the reign of Philip III were composed," he says, "out of material I had collected in order to write a novel, but which for certain reasons I never wrote."[9] In *Don Fernando*, thus, the perspective is altered. Ironic observation of character is no longer the chief motive. The emphasis is on the study of the various aspects of Spanish life of the Golden Age—its art, philosophy, religion, and culture.

For the student of Maugham's works, his travel books present several interesting and fruitful lines of critical investigation. Among the chief influences that have shaped Maugham's literary personality, that of travel is, as noted earlier, not the least significant.

The travel books of Maugham reveal the same literary personality at work that is seen in his novels and plays— the same shrewd and ironic observer of human character who aims at passionless detachment and is yet compelled, at least during some moments, to bring his sympathies into play. This observer is more interested in human nature than in places or in ideas. The forte of Maugham's travel books, therefore, is the rich display of personality types—both European and Asiatic.

Maugham's sketches of European types belong to different stations in life and to different professions. It is a motley crowd comprising missionaries, bank managers, consuls, businessmen, sailors, beachcombers, doctors, scholars, and spinsters. On closer inspection, however, the crowd sorts itself out into some definite archetypes: Among these are the "Pukka Sahib" of the Kiplingesque kind who takes pride in not knowing the language of the foreign land where he has had to live for two decades; the

[9] Revised ed., vi.

self-styled "Socialist" who, hurrying to slake his intellectual thirst by reading the latest book by Bertrand Russell, must kick his rickshaw boy because the latter does not go fast enough; the misguided man of God who loathes the Oriental from the bottom of his heart and yet must be affectionate towards him as a matter of duty; the Englishman who dreams of settling down in his motherland after a long stay abroad, but who finds, when his dream is fulfilled, that he has now become a stranger to his own country; another, who loves and lives with a native girl and has to face a difficult problem when she demands to be legally married.

Among the women in the group also we can discern certain specific types: the husband-hunting spinster; the missionary lady whose whole attitude toward life and whose conversation are one huge platitude; the English girl married to a Chinaman who, she soon discovers, is already much-married, and so on.

All these characters illustrates Maugham's eye for the oddities of human nature and his faculty of detached, ironic observation. But as in his novels, here also Maugham's sympathy breaks through time and again, and the result is a few character sketches which stand out in bold relief against the general background of portraits ironically drawn: Such, for example, are the mother superior who has "the gentlest voice I ever heard," and who, as she fondles the children in the orphanage, makes Maugham marvel "when I saw the love that filled her kind eyes and the affectionate sweetness of her smile";[10] the French nun who practices a God-like tolerance; and the Italian priest who, in spite of his limitations, has a real sense of vocation.

Occasionally, ironic observations and genuine sympathy are blended, as in the portrait of Mrs. Fanning, the "little, grotesque, ugly, housewife with a big nose and bad teeth. She was a caricature and you could not help smiling when you

[10] *On a Chinese Screen*, 159.

133

looked at her."[11] Thus speaks the ironic observer, but he is soon silenced by the voice of sympathy and admiration which remarks conclusively, "I do not think a thought of self ever entered her untidy head. She was a miracle of unselfishness. It was really hardly human."[12]

The same dualism is to be seen in Maugham's portraits of Oriental types of character, though, on the whole, the writer's sympathy and understanding seem to have the upper hand here: Thus, the Malayan guide whose attitude towards the English visitor is a combination of the schoolteacher's and the slave driver's; the Chinese professor of comparative modern literature who thinks Chinese philosophers insignificant because they lived a very long time ago; and the Chinese philosopher, the greatest authority in China on the Confucian learning, who frequents brothels—these sketches are satirical in intent. But Maugham also observes with evident admiration the vigorous young Kaw of Burma and the strong and full-blooded stripling of China; and the sight that impresses him most in India is not the Taj Mahal, but the toiling peasant.[13] The Chinese coolie fills him with "a useless compassion."[14]

"I have not the kind of intelligence that moves easily among abstractions,"[15] observed Maugham. His travel books conclusively illustrate the truth of this statement. The travel books of Huxley provide an excellent foil to those of Maugham from this point of view. In these we find at work an extremely alert and active mind with an amazingly wide range of interests —a mind more interested in ideas than in persons or places for their own sake.

In Huxley's travel books the reader ranges over the world

[11] *Ibid.*, 116.
[12] *Ibid.*, 117.
[13] *A Writer's Notebook*, 290.
[14] *Ibid.*, 69.
[15] *The Gentleman in the Parlour*, 176.

in company with a philosopher, a social thinker, an art critic, a literary critic, a historian, and a shrewd and witty Englishman of the twentieth century—all rolled into one. While traveling through France, Huxley cannot but ponder over the sociological and historical implications of the fact that France is under-populated and continues to be so.[16] While in India, his mind is continually busy drawing comparisons between the West and the East in points of philosophy of life, art, and culture.[17] While Maugham is content with oblique irony in citing a Burmese fairy tale,[18] Huxley refers, in dealing with the same subject, to Scaliger and Bentley, and remembers that "In America . . . there are still people who can discuss the first chapter of Genesis . . . with all the earnest gravity of Burmese pandits discussing the Sun Prince."[19]

The difference is even better illustrated when the two authors write about the well-known Shwe Dagon pagoda in Burma. Huxley's is the eye of the keen student of architecture, noting "the merry-go-round of architecture and decoration."[20] Maugham is more interested in the old man who lights "a row of candles before an image of the Buddha."[21] A visit to Guate-mala City prompts Huxley to compare the new edition of the *Encyclopaedia Britannica* with the old.[22] Books do not primarily interest Maugham, unless, as in the old book which Don Fernando sells him, it brings him in contact with human na-ture.[23] He prefers playing patience to reading.[24]

Reflections on philosophy, art, life, and the world—as

16 *Along the Road,* 58–63.
17 *Jesting Pilate, passim.*
18 *The Gentleman in the Parlour,* 185–97.
19 *Jesting Pilate,* 171.
20 *Ibid.,* 160.
21 *The Gentleman in the Parlour,* 11.
22 *Beyond the Maxique Bay,* 114–17.
23 *Don Fernando,* chap. ii.
24 *The Gentleman in the Parlour,* 85.

well as social and art criticism—are not indeed absent from Maugham's travel books, but with a few exceptions, like the comparison between Lamb and Hazlitt,[25] they unfortunately lean heavily on the side of triteness. His observations on the problem of evil and the Hindu doctrine of *Karma* remind one of passages in *The Summing Up* which clearly betray the lack of subtlety in Maugham's thought processes.[26] When he speaks at some length about Spanish mysticism, we are all the time conscious of the writer's not being quite in his element.[27]

In the preface to *The Gentleman in the Parlour*, Maugham speaks about the difference between the style of novel and that of the travel book.

> In a novel the style is necessarily influenced by the matter and a homogeneous manner of writing is hardly practical. . . . But if you like language for its own sake, if it amuses you to string words together in the order that most pleases you, so as to produce an effect of beauty, the essay or the book of travel gives you an opportunity. Here prose must be cultivated for its own sake.[28]

The prose that Maugham cultivates for its own sake in most of his travel books reveals, however, both the limitations and the strong points of the style of his novels. Here, as in the novels, Maugham seems to aim at lucidity, simplicity, and euphony.[29] Here too, he uses what John Brophy aptly calls the "talker's manner."[30] The strongest point of his style here also is its trenchant irony. The limitations of Maugham's style—its lack of poetry and of imaginative sweep—are not overcome in the travel books, as he himself admitted.

[25] *Ibid.*, 1–3.
[26] *Ibid.*, 176–80.
[27] *Don Fernando*, chap. x.
[28] *The Gentleman in the Parlour*, vii–viii.
[29] *The Summing Up*, 31.
[30] *Somerset Maugham*, 24.

Though I have travelled much, I am a bad traveller. The good traveller has the gift of surprise. He is perpetually interested by the differences he finds between what he knows at home and what he sees abroad. . . . But I take things for granted so quickly that I cease to see anything unusual in my new surroundings.[31]

Not thus did Borrow wander through the wild regions of Spain. The result is that Maugham's best descriptions are those which show the realist in him to advantage, as, for example, in the description of the opium den in *On a Chinese Screen* which, he finds, is a cheerful spot, homelike and cosy, and not at all the squalid and mysterious house of sin of popular imagination, or as in the description of the jungle in *The Gentleman in the Parlour* which is noted to be filled with a tremendous din, and not with silence as is commonly thought. But when he attempts poetic description as in the passage on the Great Wall of China, the reader has the uneasy feeling that the writer is talking with his tongue in his cheek.

Maugham's similes reveal little imagination. For him, the pagodas loom "huge, remote and mysterious, out of the mist of the early morning like the vague recollections of a fantastic dream."[32] Little clouds in the sky look like "fishing boats becalmed towards evening."[33]

These limitations notwithstanding, Maugham's travel books are written in an extremely lucid, readable, and graceful style of which he is a master. He talks with homely ease with his readers and keeps them interested throughout.

Another interesting line of approach to Maugham's travel books is to find out how they provide material for some of his novels, short stories, and plays. On taking up *The Painted Veil* after reading *On a Chinese Screen*, the reader gets the un-

31 *The Gentleman in the Parlour*, 12.
32 *Ibid.*, 16.
33 *On a Chinese Screen*, 173.

mistakable feeling of "I have been here before." The mother superior in the novel has already appeared in the travel book, and so also has Dr. Saunders of *The Narrow Corner*. The connection between *The Gentleman in the Parlour* and the several short stories with the background of Malaya is equally plain. Guy of "The Force of Circumstance" is only Masterson of *The Gentleman in the Parlour* placed in a complication which is suggested in the history of latter character and is worked out fully in that of the former. Similarly, both *Catalina* and *Then and Now* owe a great deal to *Don Fernando*, and possibly something to *The Land of the Blessed Virgin*.

As a writer of travel books where does Maugham stand in the illustrious fraternity headed by Sterne? One may indeed look in vain to Maugham for the delightful whimsicality of Sterne, the engaging confidences of Stevenson, Borrow's passion for the romantic, Kinglake's air of the cultured Englishman abroad, the brilliant byplay of the intellect in Huxley, Lawrence's love of beauty and his ability to bring it home to the reader, and the epic sweep and antique flavor of C. M. Doughty. But every writer has the right to be tested by the strongest link in his chain. Once we concede that right to Maugham, as indeed we must, it would be difficult for us to discover a more penetrating and shrewd observer of human nature among the writers of travel books than Maugham, with the possible exception of Graham Greene, whose interests, in his travel books, are virtually the same as Maugham's. If the test of a successful travel book is its power to enrich the reader's experience of life and the world, Maugham's travel books satisfy the test in their own way, even if they do not distill the aroma of distant lands.

For the student of Maugham, the travel books throw an interesting sidelight on the enigmatic mixture of cynicism and sympathy in him, because, in them, the reader travels through the land of Maugham's literary personality, and what he observes here reminds him of many familiar sights and landmarks that he has already seen in the novels and plays. Above all, there is not a dull moment for the reader who travels with Maugham, whether to China or Burma or Spain, for there is a "third who walks always" beside him. This "third" is none other than Meredith's Comic Spirit which looks "humanely malign" and casts "an oblique light" on the motley crowd it surveys.

CHAPTER TEN

Maugham and Love

.

Love, as E. M. Forster[1] points out, occupies an inordinately prominent place in the life of Homofictus, though its role in the life of Homo sapiens is not surely as all-absorbing. Hence, an author's attitude toward love is most often a test of his view of the world and of human nature. That is why a study of Maugham's attitude toward love is essential in an appraisal of his work. Moreover, love, sex, and marital infidelity were Maugham's favorite themes. Hence the need to study how the twin strains of cynicism and humanitarianism molded Maugham's outlook on love.

Maugham wrote about love in the concluding portions of *The Summing Up* (pp. 312–14). "Love," he remarked, "has two meanings, love pure and simple, sexual love, namely; and loving-kindness." This latter quality is described as "the better part of goodness," "the heavenly love of Plato," and in it, Maugham believed, "the sexual instinct is sublimated." As for love in the first sense, it depends, Maugham said, "on certain secretions of the sexual glands; and in the immense majority, these do not continue indefinitely to be excited by the same object and with advancing years they atrophy." Hence, "love passes, love dies. The great tragedy of life is not that men perish, but that they cease to love." The happiness love brings "may be the greatest of which man is capable, but it is seldom, seldom

[1] *Aspects of the Novel*, 76.

unalloyed . . . . Many have resented its power and angrily prayed to be delivered from its burden. They have hugged their chains, but knowing they were chains hated them too." Affection is not love, though it is often mistaken for the latter. "Love is not always blind and there are few things that cause greater wretchedness than to love with all your heart someone who you know is unworthy of love." Most of these conclusions can well be illustrated from Maugham's works.

It must be admitted, at the outset, that the general view of love which emerges from a first impression of Maugham's work is one that strongly savors of cynicism. An important reason, one suspects, of the popularity of Maugham's books is what may be called their "sexiness." "You talk as though bed were the aim and end of life," says a character in Maugham.[2] One is sometimes strongly tempted to apply the remark to Maugham himself.

More often than not, Maugham seemed to have regarded love as mere animal passion, as something purely physical, in short, as mere lust. It is this attitude that brands books like *The Painted Veil, Theatre, Up at the Villa, East of Suez,* and *Then and Now* with a repelling sordidness. The protagonists of all these books seem to think that love consists of performing the sex act as often as and whenever possible; and it is significant that four of these protagonists are women. Thus, when Julia (*Theatre*) thinks of love, she can only think of "Tom's slim, youthful body against hers, his warm nakedness and the peculiar feel of his lips, and the smell of his curly hair,"[3] and of nothing else. We are told that she falls in love with Tom, whom she hardly knows, when he rapes her, and her test of having fallen out of love is when she performs the sex act with him in a dispassionate manner. This and this alone is love for Julia.

[2] Mary Panton in *Up at the Villa,* 29.
[3] Page 206.

In a similar way Kitty (*The Painted Veil*) and Daisy (*East of Suez*) "go to it" again and again like bitches in heat, and that alone is ecstasy to them. Mary Panton's idea of bringing love into a lonely refugee's life is to play the harlot gratis to him for a single night (*Up at the Villa*). After this, it is not strange that Maugham's Machiavelli (*Then and Now*) should think of love only as a tiresome itch which much be scratched, but not at the cost of the business of the state. What is more surprising is that Larry, who has received the illumination (*The Razor's Edge*), should think of love in a very similar way. For Larry, too, love is an appetite which deserves occasional satisfaction, but it is significant that in his pattern of the ideal life love has no place. Isabel, in the same novel, loves her husband so much because "he's wonderful in bed." That does not, however, prevent her from being almost hypnotized at the sight of Larry's "long delicate, but powerful hand," which makes her face "a mask of lust."[4] Even Romance is unable to lift Maugham's conception of love above earthiness. This is how he describes Catalina's passion for her lover:

> She was breathless with lust for the male. She was like one possessed. There was something not quite human about her, something even slightly horrible, but so powerful that it was terrifying. It was sex, nothing but sex, violent and irresistible, sex in its awful nakedness.[5]

This preoccupation with the body, with sex rather than love, may well be compared and contrasted with that in D. H. Lawrence. Lawrence too exalts the physical and the animal at the expense of the spiritual. He has a morbid obsession for nakedness. He condemns men because *"Like any snake slipping into its bed of dead leaves You hurry into your clothes."*[6] His

[4] Page 169.
[5] *Catalina*, 187–88.
[6] D. H. Lawrence, *Complete Poems*, Vol. I, 246.

heroines always go into raptures over the naked bodies of the men they love. Thus, for Lady Crystabel, Annable is a "Greek statue"; and the sight of the "perfect, white, solitary nudity" of Mellors, the gamekeeper, is for Lady Chatterley "a visionary experience" which hits "her in the middle of the body" for, it is "not the stuff of beauty . . . not even the body of beauty, but a lambency, the warm, white flame of a single life, revealing itself in contours that one might touch: a body."[7]

In *Women in Love*, two men wrestle naked together till one of them swoons away, because "we are mentally, spiritually intimate; therefore we ought to be more or less physically intimate."[8] The suggestion of a homosexual idea here is again repeated in *Aaron's Rod*, where Lilly insists on rubbing the reluctant Aaron's body with oil, and Lawrence describes the operation with needless detail and obvious relish. The detailed descriptions of sexual fulfilment in Lawrence are, as Middleton Murry points out, "strangely wearisome. The sexual atmosphere is suffocating."[9] Yet, in spite of all this, Lawrence can hardly be accused of being sordid and vulgar in his view of love. This is so because Lawrence is not a mere purveyor of sex, but the prophet and philosopher of sex. There is much of the sensual and the animal in Lawrence, but when he is at his best, it is purged of its grossness by being transformed into the mysticism of sex. "I always labour at the same thing," said he, "to make the sex relation valid and precious, instead of shameful."[10]

Sex had a definite place in Lawrence's idea of life, which was the return to "the natural man." This return could be made only through the senses, hence the exaltation of the animal over the spiritual; and woman, as being nearer to Nature than man, was the instrument with the help of which this return could be

[7] *Lady Chatterley's Lover*, 79.
[8] *Birkin to Crich, Women in Love*, 286.
[9] *Son of Woman, The story of D. H. Lawrence*, 364.
[10] *Selected Literary Criticism* (ed. by A. Beal), 23.

made. "In the flesh, in woman," he wrote in the preface to *Sons and Lovers*, "we know God the Father, the Inscrutable, the Unknowable." Hence he saw the sex act as a mystical experience which brought man into immediate contact with reality. Thus, sex in Lawrence is firmly grounded in a serious philosophy of life and is purged of all earthiness by being enveloped in a mystical grandeur. Nothing of the kind happens in Maugham. Love as sex, in the illustrations from his works given earlier, remains rooted to the physical plane, and there is nothing which can lift it higher.

A comparison of Maugham with Huxley also reveals differences. In Huxley's earlier books, too, love is viewed in a cynical way as a merely physical process. The obvious cynicism of *The Fifth Philosopher's Song*[11] may be an example of sheer flippancy, but the picture of love in his earlier novels is definitely cynical. Love is viewed here merely as a matter of hormones. It is, at its highest, "a decent, good-humoured, happy sensuality."[12] Huxley's characters seem to believe that at its worst, sex is only the last refuge of the bored and the weary. But in Huxley we are all the time conscious of a definite feeling of sex-disgust, which makes him paint love as he does, and it is well known how Huxley turned from cynicism to mysticism in his later works. In Maugham's pictures of the animal passion in Julia and Kitty, however, it is difficult to find any evidence of a feeling of sex repulsion which prompts the author to paint them as they are. The animal passion is painted with obvious relish, which leads one to suspect that the author is convinced that this alone is love.

The "sexiness" of Maugham's works is nearer to that of Maupassant and Zola. The work of either of these French writers is, at its worst, marred by a taint of sordidness which

[11] *Rotunda*, 706–709.
[12] *Point Counter Point*, 28.

arises out of viewing love merely as desire. Zola, as an avowed naturalist, saw only the human animal. The novelist, he claimed, was only a scientist, observing, experimenting, and recording his findings. Since the soul was an entity amenable neither to observation nor to experiment, it was promptly denied. Hence Zola's studies of human passion, though marked by minute observation and realism, remain, at their worst, hopelessly one-sided. Maupassant is no doubt more aware of the finer aspect of love, as is seen from memorable stories like "Two Soldiers" and "Clochette." Yet, as a confirmed pessimist and bohemian, he is, more often than not, preoccupied with the animal side of love. About Maupassant, Maugham himself writes in the preface to *Altogether*: "He was obsessed by the tiresome notion, common then to his countrymen, that it was a duty a man owed himself to hop into bed with every woman under forty that he met"[13]—a remark which, with some variation, may be applied to some of Maugham's own characters.

Moreover, of all the manifestations of love, Maugham seemed to be most interested in adultery. There are very few of his books in which the subject of marital infidelity, especially in woman, does not enter. Maugham's attitude to adultery also savors of cynicism. As noted earlier, in stories like "Virtue," and "The Book-bag," in plays like *East of Suez,* and in novels like *The Painted Veil,* the fact of adultery is recorded and presented with a cynical indifference to moral values. It is not that the author had so staunch a faith in love as to hold, with Browning, that love could never be immoral unless it is false to itself. Maugham's preoccupation with adultery did not seem to spring from a conviction that it is impossible for love to be a sin, even when it is unlawful, for love was identified with mere physical pleasure and was devoid of any spiritual content for most of his adulterous characters. There is no resisting the conclusion,

[13] Page x.

therefore, that the harping on the subject of adultery in Maugham was motivated by a rather cheap desire to sneer at traditional ethics, and as such it lies open to the charge of cynicism, of which such sneering is an essential mark.

But there are other facets of Maugham's view of love which show love in a better light and reveal his sympathy for those who suffer in love—not in sexual affairs alone—though these facets are perhaps less obvious than the "sexiness" and the cynical treatment of adultery. Thus, many of his lovers find to their dismay that love is a cruel spell, a *Belle Dame Sans Merci* which holds them in thrall and torments them and which is by no means a source of joy and peace. This is how the coming of love to Philip is described:

> He had thought of love as a rapture which seized one so that all the world seemed Spring-like, he had looked forward to an ecstatic happiness; but this was not happiness, it was a hunger of the soul, it was a painful yearning, it was a bitter anguish he had never known before.[14]

"It is awful, love, isn't it?" he asks, "Fancy any one wanting to be in love."[15] And the story of how Philip struggles, and struggles in vain, to free himself from the bondage of passion is told with deep sympathy.

When Beatriz (*Catalina*) realizes that she is in love with Blasco, she feels "a sharp pain in her heart, as though it were pierced with a sword."[16] That moment settles her doom. She knows that the object of her love is unattainable and renounces the world to become a hard and domineering prioress. But the wound is never completely healed. Years later, the memory of that love comes back to her, and the hard and proud Dona Beatriz bursts into tears. A fine definition of love occurs in *The*

14 *Of Human Bondage*, 295.
15 *Ibid.*, 393.
16 Page 59.

Breadwinner, where Charles Battle, who is leaving his snobbish wife, tells her, "If you still had for me that hungry craving of the soul they call love, I think it's possible I shouldn't have the courage to leave you."[17] "We can't love because we ought to. Love comes and goes and we can none of us help ourselves,"[18] murmurs Maurice pathetically in *The Sacred Flame*. "I couldn't resist the love that swept me up, as a gust of wind in March sweeps up last year's dead leaf,"[19] cries Stella in the same play. "I don't offer you peace and quietness," says Elizabeth's lover to her in *The Circle*, "I offer you unrest and anxiety. I don't offer you happiness. I offer you love."[20] There is an undercurrent of pity for the suddenness with which love seizes Violet and Knobby Clarke in the otherwise cynical story, "The Back of Beyond." They "lived on terms of close intimacy for three years before they fell in love with one another. Neither saw love approaching." Suddenly, one day, they realize that they are in love with each other.

> When they met next day neither referred to what had happened, but each knew that something inevitable had passed. They behaved to one another as they had always done, they continued to behave so for weeks, but they felt that everything was different.[21]

Maugham is full of commiseration for lovers, not only because love is a cruel force which brings pain and anguish, but also because he seems to believe that it is nevertheless beautiful, with a beauty that is so very short lived. Maugham's lovers sometimes exult when they find themselves free from the bondage of love. It is such a relief at first. But they soon realize that

17 *Collected Plays*, Vol. II, 289.
18 *Ibid.*, Vol. III, 241.
19 *Ibid.*, 312.
20 *Ibid.*, Vol. II, 87.
21 *The Complete Short Stories*, Vol. III, 1175.

there is now a void in their hearts which nothing can fill. That is the experience of Bertha Craddock and Philip Carey. "The tragedy of love is not death or separation," says Neilson in "Red," "The tragedy of love is that love dies,"[22] and the tragedy is made more poignant by the fact "that the essential element of love is a belief in its own eternity."[23] Hence, commenting on the young lovers in *The Razor's Edge*, Maugham remarked:

> There is nothing more touching than the sight of young love, and I, a middle-aged man then, envied them, but at the same time, I couldn't imagine why, I felt sorry for them. It was silly because, so far as I know, there was no impediment to their happiness.[24]

"It only comes once in a lifetime, love like that,"[25] says Mrs. Miller, wistfully looking upon her young daughter in love. The lovers in "The Colonel's Lady" have been happy because, "he died in the full flush of his first love and had never known that love so seldom endures; he had only known its bliss and beauty. In her own bitter grief she found solace in the thought that he'd been spared all sorrow."[26]

But the sorrows of lovers do not end here. Another frequent thought in Maugham is that love reaps the harvest of grief alone, for it is so many times one-sided. "Of course I knew you never loved me as much as I loved you," says Norah to the unfortunate Philip who cannot respond, because on him is laid the cruel spell of Mildred. "I'm afraid that's always the case," moans Philip, "There's always one who loves and one who lets himself be loved."[27] Lydia's confession about her love for her worthless husband is equally significant.

[22] *Ibid.*, 1531.
[23] *Ibid.*, 1526.
[24] Page 16.
[25] *Sheppey, Collected Plays*, Vol. III, 228.
[26] *The Complete Short Stories*, Vol. II, 1687.
[27] *Of Human Bondage*, 366.

He's cruel and selfish, unscrupulous and wicked. I don't care.
I don't respect him, I don't trust him, but I love him; I love him
with my body, with my thoughts, with my feelings, with everything that's me. . . . I can't imagine anything more heart-rending
than to love with all your soul someone that you know is
worthless.[28]

The roles are reversed in *The Painted Veil*, where Walter, the
injured husband, tells his frivolous wife:

I had no illusions about you. I knew you were silly and frivolous
and emptyheaded. But I loved you . . . . I knew that you'd only
married me for convenience. I loved you so much, I didn't care
. . . I was thankful to be allowed to love you.[29]

Even the tiresome Gwen, in *For Services Rendered*, becomes for
a moment a pathetic figure when she cries, "Oh, it's so awful to
love someone with all your heart and to know that the very
sight of you maddens him beyond endurance."[30] The narrator's
comment on Jack Almond's pathetic end in "A Casual Affair"
is, "I know nothing more shattering than to love with all your
heart, than not to be able however hard you try to break yourself
of it, someone who you know is worthless."[31] Neilson, in "Red,"
is glad because he has seen a miracle:

With two lovers there is always one who loves and one who lets
himself be loved; it is a bitter truth to which most of us have to
resign ourselves; but now and then there are two who love and
two who let themselves be loved. Then one might fancy that the
sun stands still as it stood when Joshua prayed to the God
of Israel.[32]

In spite of the "sexiness" of some of his books, Maugham

28 *Christmas Holiday*, 276.
29 Page 73.
30 *Collected Plays*, Vol. III, 174.
31 *The Complete Short Stories*, Vol. III, 1513.
32 *Ibid.*, 1523.

is not aware of the finer side of love. This is specially to be seen in some of his later works, where his temperament has acquired a greater mellowness. The early story "Red" does indeed lift love up from mere animal passion, as Neilson waxes almost lyrical in describing the love of those two handsome young things—Red and Sally.

> That is the real love, not the love that comes from sympathy, common interests, or intellectual community, but love pure and simple. That is the love that Adam felt for Eve when he awoke and found her in the garden gazing at him with dewy eyes. That is the love that draws the beasts to one another, and the Gods, that is the love that makes the world a miracle.[33]

But it is only in the later years that the realization that love need not die, though youth dies—that young love may be transformed into something richer and finer with age—seems to have come to Maugham. The sad and wise Mrs. Tabret, who speaks for the author in *The Sacred Flame*, voices the sentiment in describing her son and his wife:

> They had loved one another as two healthy young things love. Their love was deep and passionate, but it was rooted in sex. It might have come about with time that it would have acquired a more spiritual character, it might have been that the inevitable trials of life endured together would have given birth to an affection, and a confidence in one another that might have given a new glow to the fading fires of passion.[34]

"Sanatorium," a later story, is, as noted earlier, a touching account of the love that inspires two invalids who are doomed to die and who have now something worthwhile to live for, during the short span of life remaining to them.

The question of how Maugham's attitude toward love has

[33] *Ibid.*, 1523.
[34] *The Collected Plays.* Vol. III, 295.

been molded by his life and his personality is obviously a delicate one. A few broad suggestions based strictly on Maugham's own account of himself may, however, be made with due apologies. Thus, it is possible to trace the "sexiness" of some of Maugham's books back to his early life when, as an adolescent, he was starved of affection. An excess of affection on the part of his mother, in his adolescence, warped D. H. Lawrence's whole attitude toward love, though he was later able to sublimate his mother-fixation. Where Lawrence suffered from plenty, Maugham seems to have suffered from want, with a similar result. But unlike Lawrence, Maugham was not able to formulate a philosophy of sex. In *The Summing Up*, Maugham said:

> The keenest pleasure to which the body is susceptible is that of sexual congress. I have known men who gave up their whole lives to this. It has been my misfortune that a native fastidiousness has prevented me from indulging as much in this particular delight as I might have. I have exercised moderation because I was hard to please.[35]

In his books, Maugham has not been hard to please. Then again, Maugham's idea of love as an evil spell producing anguish, as a mad fury, is most completely developed in the picture of Mildred in *Of Human Bondage*; of Mildred, says R. A. Cordell, "one is permitted to say only that she is not altogether a creature of the novelist's fancy."[36]

One may also recall the facts about Maugham's married life as recorded in the account of his personal life discussed earlier in chapter ii. In *The Summing Up*, Maugham wrote:

> Though I have been in love a good many times I have never experienced the bliss of requited love. I know that it is the best thing that life can offer and it is a thing that almost all men, though perhaps only for a short time, have enjoyed. I have most

[35] Page 33.
[36] W. *Somerset Maugham*, 94.

loved people who cared little or nothing for me and when
people have loved me I have been embarrassed. It has been a
predicament that I have not quite known how to deal with. . . .
I have tried, with gentleness when possible, and if not, with irritation, to escape from the trammels with which their love
bound me. I have been jealous of my independence. I am incapable of complete surrender.[37]

This confession explains much in Maugham's view of love as
expressed in his books.

Maugham's attitude toward love as revealed in his works
thus shows the influence of both the strains of cynicism and
humanitarianism. It was cynical in the sense that many times
Maugham was preoccupied with the merely animal aspect of
love, which results in a cynical denial of one of the fundamental
values of life. Maugham's preoccupation with adultery lies open
to the same charge. But not always did Maugham identify love
with mere sex and adultery. When, with years, his temperament
became more mellow, he seemed to become more and more
aware of other and finer facets of love. Moreover, because
Maugham viewed love as a cruel spell which torments men and
women, his sympathies were deeply stirred by the unfortunate
victims. He saw them suffer because the joy of love is ultimately
sorrow, because love is beautiful, but "beauty vanishes, beauty
passes," and because in love there is always one who loves and
one who lets himself be loved.

Various writers have viewed love each in his own way.
There is, first of all, the eminently normal and sane attitude
toward love as exemplified by lovers in the novels of the level-
headed Jane Austen. The heroes of Scott, those shadowy per-
fections of manhood, and his heroines, those abstractions of
beauty and virtue, illustrate love as seen through the rosy
spectacles of chivalry. Shelley mostly saw love as the mating of

[37] Page 53.

two souls alone, while with Zola and Maupassant, the pendulum swung to the other extreme of restricting love to mere physical contact. With Meredith and Browning, earth and Heaven meet halfway, and love is both a divine companionship and a sharing of the experiences of practical life together. Love is identified with sex in Lawrence, but sex itself is bathed in a mystic effulgence, while for the earlier Huxley and for Swift, sex in its gross nakedness arouses disgust and repulsion.

The majority of these writers had what may be called a definite philosophy of love, a well-organized outlook on love. The same, perhaps, cannot be said of Maugham, though suggestions of such an outlook are scattered throughout his work. Maugham's view of love was, on the whole, woefully devoid of romance and all that that term conveys. Maugham's chief limitation—his lack of poetry and emotional intensity—is again in evidence in his attitude toward love. It is perhaps all these limitations, together with the "sexiness" and the preoccupation with adultery in some of his books, that give a certain air of cheapness and superficiality to Maugham's pictures of love on the whole, though love is the chief theme of his works.

CHAPTER ELEVEN

Literary Technique

.

I T IS A TRUISM that an artist's outlook on life and his technique are so intimately connected with each other that they are inseparable in all but theory. In general, one may say that the literary technique of a writer is determined and shaped chiefly by his outlook on life. Maugham's literary technique must therefore be examined in the light of the conflict between his cynicism and humanitarianism.

The chief influences which shaped Maugham's literary personality were, it may be recalled, those of his unhappy childhood and adolescence, travel, and the French models which Maugham followed in the days of his apprenticeship. The first of these influences, which was perhaps responsible for Maugham's deep sensibility and filled him with a dread of sentiment, often led to a hard detachment; the second contributed to the variety of scene and character and also to the habit of "amused tolerance"; the third influenced his literary technique by providing both precept and example.

It is interesting to see how Maugham's literary technique was determined and shaped by the genesis of his literary personality. As Maugham tells us in *The Summing Up*,[1] he took the objective realism of Maupassant as his model when he started his literary career with *Liza of Lambeth*. But he soon developed an individual technique which was expressive of his own

[1] Chapter two.

personality. The salient features of his technique may now be indicated. First, it includes a "detached observer" of life and of human nature. This suggests objective realism pure and simple, but Maugham's technique is not completely objective. It is in a sense subjective also, for the "detached observer" does not remain completely aloof, nor does he remain outside the circumference of his narrative. He himself is a character in the story, the events of which are viewed through his eyes and narrated through his lips. Now, this narrator evidently represents the author, and thus Maugham's personal point of view, the "first person singular" (which forms the title of one of his books) colors the whole story. Also, this observer frequently forgets his detachment. His sense of irony is sharp, and it is generally brought into play. Moreover, his native sensibility, though effectively suppressed, occasionally breaks through. Last of all, this observer has, partly by nature and partly as a result of the influence of his literary models, a sense of form and construction, as well as a lucid style.

The excellences of this literary technique are many. It provides realism, the fruit of minute observation of the world and of human nature. Travel has sharpened this power of observation and has supplied a great variety of scene and setting for Maugham's narratives. Further, the use of the device of the "first person singular" secures verisimilitude and plausibility. The reader gets the impression that the writer is personally talking to him from his own experience, and the impression goes a long way in creating in the reader's mind an illusion of the truthfulness of the story and the characters. The sharp sense of irony is an obvious advantage in the delineation of foibles in the portrayal of the social scene and human character. The sense of form and construction ensures that the story is well told and pointed, with a beginning, a middle, and an end clearly discernible, while the lucid style makes for readability and popular appeal.

In the field of the drama, where the "detached observer" obviously cannot appear, the flair for irony receives full scope and enables Maugham to continue the tradition of the comedy of manners. Owing to his sense of form, the management of situation and conflict is skillful, and his lucid and informal style makes his dramatic dialogue appear easy and natural.

But with all these excellences, this literary technique labors under severe limitations, as indicated earlier in the survey of Maugham's works. These limitations are many. The technique of the detached observer who exercises his sense of irony is no doubt of capital utility in the treatment of certain themes, such as those which involve social and personal satire. But the danger inherent in it is that the attitude of ironical detachment may easily degenerate into one of cynical indifference and lack of warmth.

Realism, too, has its own pitfalls, of which Zola provides a glaring example. The creed of extreme realism made Zola revel in sordidness for its own sake and made his picture of life as hopelessly one-sided as the romantic vision which he attacked. Moreover, the cult of neatness and severity of form and construction and of clarity and straightforwardness of style may well conceal a lack of suggestive overtones and of imaginative flights.

The greatest limitation of Maugham's technique is the one which is inherent in his variation of the method of narration in the first person singular, where the detached observer is a character in the story itself. With all its advantages, this method has its own defects. Not only does it unnecessarily restrict Maugham's vision—for he gives up here the writer's birthright of omniscience—but it also seems to encourage superficiality by making it impossible for him to go deep into the minds of his characters, to fathom their secrets, or to share their emotional turmoils. It seems to preclude, consequently, all depth from Maugham's picture of life and of character, and the lack of this depth is most seriously felt when the author is trying to deal with the serious issues of life. It may be argued that the method of narration in the first person singular has been used with great success in some of the finest novels in the world, e.g., *Moby Dick, David Copperfield,* and *The Master of Ballantrae,* but there is an important difference betwen their method and Maugham's. The narrators in these novels do not try to remain aloof and indifferent, nor shirk the responsibility of plunging into the thick of the conflict. In Maugham he does both, and hence Maugham's variation of this method lies open to this charge.

A survey of the three chief forms handled by Maugham, viz., the novel, drama, and the short story, can now be made from the point of view of his technique.

THE NOVEL

"After pursuing the art of fiction for over forty years," says Maugham, "I have a notion that I know a good deal more about it than most people."[2] Maugham's conception of the novel is set forth in *The Summing Up* and in the first chapter, "The Art of Fiction," of his book *Ten Novels and their Authors.* He tells us in *The Summing Up* that:

> As a writer of fiction I go back, through innumerable generations, to the teller of tales round the fire in the cavern that sheltered neolithic men. I have had some sort of story to tell, and it has interested me to tell it. To me it has been a sufficient object in itself.[3]

He is convinced that "the aim of the writer of fiction is not to

[2] *The Mixture as Before,* vii.
[3] Page 155.

instruct, but to please."[4] "I think it an abuse to use the novel as a pulpit or a platform," he adds, "and I believe readers are misguided when they suppose they can thus easily acquire knowledge."[5]

The qualities that a good novel should have, according to Maugham, are:

> It should have a widely interesting theme ... so broadly human that its appeal is to men and women in general ... and the theme should be of enduring interest. ... The story the author has to tell should be coherent and persuasive; it should have a beginning, a middle and an end ... the creatures of the novelist's invention should be observed with individuality, and their actions should proceed from their characters ... it is all the better if the characters are in themselves interesting. ... The dialogue ... should serve to characterize the speakers and advance the story. The narrative passages should be vivid, to the point, and no longer than is necessary to make the motives of the persons concerned, and the situations in which they are placed, clear and convincing. The writing should be simple enough for anyone of fair education to read with ease, and the manner should fit the matter .... Finally, a novel should be entertaining .... This is the essential quality without which no other quality avails and the more intelligent the entertainment a novel offers, the better it is.[6]

About Chekhov, Maugham states in *The Summing Up* that "he had his limitations and he very wisely made them the basis of his art."[7] It is interesting to see the same process at work in the foregoing tests of a "good" novel proposed by Maugham. His insistence on the story, on entertainment, on "a beginning, a middle and an end," and on simplicity of style—

[4] *Ten Novels and Their Authors*, 8.
[5] *Ibid.*, 7.
[6] *Ibid.*, 12–14.
[7] Page 142.

all this is highly significant. It must, however, be admitted that Maugham faithfully tried to follow all these principles in his own career as a writer of fiction.

In his first three major novels, viz., *Liza of Lambeth, Mrs. Craddock,* and *Of Human Bondage,* the characteristic Maugham technique is not followed in its entirety, nor did it ever become a cast-iron framework. Thus, all the three novels employ the omniscient method of narration in the third person, and in none of them does the "detached and ironic observer" appear. In the character of Miss Ley (*Mrs. Craddock*) there is, no doubt an early sketch of the "detached observer," but it remains only a sketch. The realism of none of these three novels is extremist or sordid. The picture of the slums in Liza is not one-sided. There is no wallowing here in squalidness for its own sake, as in Zola. The picture of love as misery in *Mrs. Craddock* and *Of Human Bondage* is not ugly, for the author's faith in love as a value and his deep sympathy are always in evidence. This sympathy also prevents the irony of the author from degenerating in these novels into cold cynicism.

In form and style, as shown earlier, these novels do not have the skill of some of the later ones. *Liza* is perhaps too sketchy, and both *Mrs. Craddock* and *Of Human Bondage* are too long to have perfection of form and construction. In all these novels, incident follows incident in a straightforward way, and there is no shifting of the story back and forth for special technical effects. The style of these early novels, though lucid and clear, seems to lack the flexibility, the ease, the rhythm, and the grace of some of Maugham's later books. On the whole, except in the matter of style and form, the limitations of Maugham's technique do not much affect his achievement in this early phase, because the technique has not yet become rigid and tyrannical.

The typical Maugham-manner is perfected in *The Moon*

and Sixpence, and its severe limitations are fully revealed here, as already shown, in the picture of Strickland, the genius. The novel has a fine compactness of form, and the construction of the narrative by bits judiciously chosen from several sources and worked up into a mosaic shows technical skill of a high order. The easy, informal style can boast of a new flexibility. Yet, the detached manner has already grown tyrannical and is responsible for the inability to probe deeper into the secret of genius which is the theme of the novel.

Cakes and Ale is a marvel of constructive skill, where the use of the "time shift" makes for variety and verisimilitude. But here, fortunately, the aloofness of the detached observer breaks down under the charm and generosity of Rosie, and the excellences of Maugham's technique are nowhere better seen, nor are its limitations less apparent than in this novel. The chief limitation of the Maugham-manner, irony and detachment leading to cynical indifference and lack of warmth, is surmounted here because of the human sympathy which Rosie evokes in the author.

But, it is in the novels of the last phase that the limitations of Maugham's literary technique are most clearly exposed. In these novels Maugham tries to grapple with the more serious issues of life. But the technique of the detached observer is thoroughly inadequate for this purpose, and its limitations, combined with those of the author's vision, lead to the superficiality of *The Razor's Edge* and *Christmas Holiday,* to the predominance of melodrama over tragedy in *The Narrow Corner,* to the cheapness of *Theatre, Up at the Villa,* and *Then and Now,* and to the pedestrian handling of romance in *Catalina.*

The limitations of the Maugham-manner are again revealed in Maugham's method of characterization, whether in the novel or in the short story. The method of the detached observer is, no doubt, useful for providing objective descriptions of characters. Maugham is fond of giving detailed descriptions of the personal appearance of his characters. This is how the hero of *The Razor's Edge* is described:

> He was . . . just under six feet, thin and loose-limbed. He was a pleasant-looking boy, neither handsome nor plain, rather shy and in no way remarkable . . . his hands . . . were long, but not large for his size, beautifully shaped and at the same time strong. . . . His face, grave in response, was tanned, but otherwise there was little colour in it, and his features, though regular enough, were undistinguished. He had rather high cheek-bones and his temples were hollow. He had dark brown hair with a slight wave in it. His eyes looked larger than they really were because they were deep set in the orbits and his lashes were thick and long. His eyes were peculiar. They were so dark that the iris made one colour with the pupil and this gave them a peculiar intensity. He had a natural grace that was attractive.[8]

In the short stories, where so much space cannot obviously be spared, Maugham is content with a smaller piece of description, as, for example, in the case of Caypor in the story "The Traitor" (*Ashenden*):

> His [Ashenden's] glance showed him a man of about forty-five with short dark hair, somewhat grizzled, of middle height, but corpulent, with a broad red clean-shaven face. He wore a shirt open at the neck, with a wide collar, and a grey suit.[9]

Maugham also tells us as much about the idiosyncrasies and the salient qualities of mind in his characters, as far as it is possible for a detached observer to know of these. Motives, as far as they are apparent to the detached observer, are also noted and explained. All this, no doubt, creates an impression of verisimilitude, and Maugham's characters are eminently convincing

[8] Page 16.
[9] Page 161.

within the framework of the narratives wherein they figure. But it is doubtful whether even the best of them have the solidity and depth which would make them great creations of artistic imagination. This is so because subtle analysis of mental processes and minute soul-probing are both out of the ken of Maugham's "detached observer."

In both Larry and Caypor, the want of this soul-probing is keenly felt. It makes the sea change in Larry appear totally artificial, and it makes the tragedy of Caypor a rather cheap story of espionage which could otherwise have attained the true tragic heights. It is only when Maugham's detachment is broken and his feelings are deeply stirred—which happens only occasionally—that he can create characters like Rosie Driffield (*Cakes and Ale*) and Philip Carey (*Of Human Bondage*), characters that are able to stir our own feelings.

Maugham's method of the detached observer succeeds better in his ironical portraits, such as Alroy Kear (*Cakes and Ale*), Captain Nichols (*The Narrow Corner*), Mortimer Ellis ("The Round Dozen"), and Mrs. Forrester ("The Creative Impulse"). But significantly enough, it was only when Maugham's sympathy qualified his irony that his most memorable satirical sketches were created, of which those of Elliott Templeton (*The Razor's Edge*) and Mr. Harrington (*Ashenden*) are fine examples.

But the destructive weapon of irony became habitual, and Maugham could not lay it aside while painting his few "good" men and women. Thus, both of the "good" men—Dick Stroeve (*The Moon and Sixpence*) and Sheppey (*Sheppey*)—fail to come to life since they cannot disarm their ironical creator and ultimately become rather farcical characters. Erik Christessen (*The Narrow Corner*), another "good" man, is not convincing because he fails to stir our sympathies, perhaps because he has not sufficiently stirred Maugham's. It is only in the early phase, when irony and detachment have not as yet engulfed Maugham's native sensibility, that we find a more successful portrait of a good man, viz., Athelny (*Of Human Bondage*).

THE SHORT STORY

Maugham wrote about his conception of the short story in the prefaces to the numerous collections of his short stories, in *The Summing Up*, and in the introduction to *Ten Novels and their Authors*. The last mentioned source gives the following definition:

> A short story is a piece of fiction that can be read, according to its length, in any thing between ten minutes and an hour, and it deals with a single, well-defined subject, an incident or a closely related series of incidents,—spiritual or material,—which is complete. It should be impossible to add to it or to take away from it.[10]

Of characterization in the short story, Maugham said, "He [the short story writer] has not room to describe and develop a character; he can only give the salient trait that brings the character to life and so make the story he has to tell plausible."[11] Maugham believed that a short story should have a definite form, a logical development, a proper beginning and a middle, and a definite point.

Here, again, it is obvious that Maugham formulated general rules based upon his own practice, which were determined by the excellences and limitations of his own powers. These were nearer to Maupassant's than to Chekhov's; hence Maugham's master in the short story was Maupassant, and the Chekhovian short story, which aims at creating a mood rather than telling a tale, was evidently not for him.

In the short stories, as indicated earlier, the detached ob-

[10] Page 14.
[11] *Creatures of Circumstance*, 4.

server in the Maugham manner forgets his aloofness more frequently than he does in the novels, especially in the last phase of Maugham's career as a writer of short stories; hence, Maugham's best stories escape the danger of cynical indifference, lack of warmth, and superficiality. A study of the form and construction of these stories reveals Maugham's technical virtuosity within the limits imposed on him by the peculiar nature of his talent.

Maugham's stories are of varying length: "Rain" is one of the longest, running up to as many as thirty-eight pages, while "Meyhew" is one of the very short short-stories from *Cosmopolitans* and occupies only three pages. But, whatever its length, a story by Maugham is most often a close-knit narrative of an event or events, characterized by clarity and coherence. There are no irrelevancies to blunt the "point" of the story, and the descriptions of places and persons are short and concise.

The stories show a wealth of dramatic situation, of which a fine example is provided by that situation in "Rain" where, after her victory over the missionary, the prostitute suddenly appears dressed in all her finery; in the management of suspense, the murder story "The Letter" can challenge the best detective stories on their own ground. In each story, the beginning and the end are managed with an unerring eye on effect. There is ample variety in the way the beginning is made. Maugham sometimes began by introducing the major characters and explaining the preliminary situation. But occasionally he began by sketching the scene of the action, as in the "Footprints in the Jungle." In some stories, the action starts straightway from the beginning, as in "The Outstation," where the conflict between Warburton and his assistant begins with the opening of the narrative itself; in others, Maugham begins "at a tangent," as in "The Book-bag." To begin a story with a confession of a personal nature, as in "Straight Flush," is another favorite method, while, occasionally, a general observation provides a starting point, as in "The Lotus Eater": "Most people, the vast majority in fact, lead the lives that circumstances have thrust upon them." Some stories, like "The Unconquered," begin in *medias res*, while the technique of the retrospect is handled with great skill in stories like "Before the Party."

The ending, too, is made in a variety of ways. It is always a "pointed" ending, but the "point" is made in different ways. It is sometimes made with a clinching comment, as at the end of "Jane"—"she *was* priceless," or with an ironical flourish, as in "Gigolo and Gigolette," or by indicating the moral, as in "The Yellow Streak." Certain stories like "Mr. Harrington's Washing" and "In a Strange Land" end on a note of climax, while a surprising turn of situation can also mark the close, as in "The Poet."

This flawlessness of form and construction and this sense of dramatic situation go a long way in making all of Maugham's stories readable, but it is only when these technical excellences are combined with human warmth that Maugham creates his most memorable stories.

THE DRAMA

Maugham's views on drama are set out at length chiefly in the prefaces to his plays, and much of what is said in these prefaces was later incorporated in *The Summing Up*. Maugham believed that "prose drama is one of the lesser arts, like wood-carving or dancing";[12] it is "the most ephemeral of all the arts. . . . No form of art has a more vivid appeal than the drama, but it is just this vividness that makes it so impermanent."[13] Maugham's argument was that the foundation of living drama is actuality, which drama has to reproduce as exactly as possible; actuality

[12] *The Collected Plays.* Vol. II, p. xviii.
[13] *Ibid.,* Vol. I, p. xviii.

consisted of the manners, the customs, the way of speech, and the thoughts and ideas of the time. But all these change and change rapidly, and hence, "the day before yesterday's newspaper is not more dead than the play of twenty years ago."

To the objection that many plays have outlived their times and are still acted, Maugham's answer was that the majority of these are poetic and "have been preserved for the loveliness of their verse rather than for their dramatic value. As to plays in prose I cannot think of a single serious one that has held the stage." The comedies that have survived, Maugham thought, are acted and seen "from a sense of duty," and "their interest is archaeological."[14]

As for the scope of drama, Maugham believed that "the drama will do best to confine itself to what it can best do. This . . . is to give pleasure by telling a story, delineating character and by stirring the emotions or causing laughter."[15] "It is not a work of edification, though it should be a work of art, and if it castigates the follies of the moment that is by the way and only in so far as this no doubt laudable process occasions laughter. The object is the entertainment of the audience, not their improvement."[16] Maugham attacks the drama of ideas with great vigor and asserts that "ideas, new or old, as such, are no concern" of the dramatist, "nor is the drama even a good vehicle for propaganda."[17]

Maugham's views about the future of realistic prose drama were pessimistic. In the preface to the last volume of his plays, written in 1931, he wrote:

the form of drama that I knew is destined to end very soon. . . . Realistic drama in prose is a form of art, though a minor one, and a minor art, responding to a particular state in civilization,

[14] *Ibid.*, Vol. I, p. xviii.
[15] *Ibid.*, Vol. II, p. xviii.
[16] *Ibid.*, Vol. II, p. ix.
[17] *Ibid.*, Vol. II, p. xvii.

is likely to perish with a change in that stage . . . . Ibsen brought the realistic prose drama to such perfection as it is capable of, and in the process killed it.[18]

Maugham believed that realistic prose drama could survive only if it turned to the allied arts of verse and music for help.

It is obvious that Maugham's idea of the nature and scope of prose drama is unnecessarily restricted. In his idea of the drama again, we find Maugham setting down rules based only upon his own powers and limitations.

Maugham is on surer ground when he speaks about his own plays. "In the drama," he says in *The Summing Up*, "I have found myself at home in the traditional moulds."[19] His plays, he tells us, "are written in the tradition which flourished so brightly in the Restoration period. . . . It is drama not of action, but of conversation. It treats with indulgent cynicism the humours, follies and vices of the world of fashion."[20]

Maugham's comedies show technical excellence of a high order, for his ironical manner is best suited to this form of art, but in his serious plays the limitations imposed upon him by his habitual use of the ironical manner are keenly felt. The comedies are, almost without exception, extremely well constructed, and Maugham's natural sense of form is nowhere else seen to better advantage than in them.

"The secret of playwriting can be given in two Maxims," writes Maugham in *The Summing Up*, "stick to the point and whenever you can, cut."[21] Any single comedy of Maugham can be cited as a practical example of both of these maxims. Each of these comedies is built round a clear-cut single plot unclogged by any minor actions. Even when the action is a complicated one, as in *Our Betters*, which presents a social panorama and

---

[18] *Ibid.*, Vol. II, p. xx.
[19] Page 150.
[20] *Ibid.*, 82–83.
[21] Page 84.

employs several characters for the purpose, the impression of unity is preserved by bringing all these characters in contact with Pearl, who towers above them all and represents the focal point of the whole picture.

Maugham has a keen eye for dramatic situation: Hence, the roaring success of farces like *Home and Beauty* and *Jack Straw*. The more substantial comedies of manners and morals, too, are rich in effective situation, of which Lady Kitty's first entry in *The Circle*, the opening situation in *Penelope*, and the incident of the handkerchiefs in *The Constant Wife* are examples picked at random. Maugham's easy and informal style is another great asset, and the dialogue in these plays is eminently natural and unforced, without being trivial. It was only later, and that too in a serious play, that Maugham attempted a greater elaboration of dialogue, making it "literary," as critics of *The Sacred Flame* rightly pointed out.

The dialogue in the comedies sparkles with wit, repartee, and epigram, though the forte of Maugham's comedy, unlike Wilde's, lies not in these but in general social satire. The wit of the early farces, like *Lady Frederick*, shows the influence of Wilde in its placing of glittering paradoxes in the mouth of almost every character. Maugham actually tells us that, when the American manager who bought the play asked him to add some more epigrams, "I went away, and in two hours wrote as I could, twenty-four."[22] The repartee in the mature comedies is of a higher order, as it is firmly rooted in character and action. Thus, when Paradine Fouldes, the cynic, remarks in *Lady Frederick* that "our relations have always such an engaging frankness: Like a bad looking-glass, they always represent you with a crooked nose and a cast in your eye,"[23] the observation is one which may safely be put in the mouth of any one of the charac-

[22] *The Collected Plays*, Vol. I, p. x.
[23] *Ibid.*, Vol. I, 54.

ters in the play. But when the counterpart of Fouldes in *The Circle*, viz., Champion-Cheney, observes that "a woman will always sacrifice herself if you give her the opportunity; it is her favourite form of self-indulgence," he makes a remark which no other character in the play can make with equal justification: it fits his character and experience like a glove.

Maugham's method of objective portrayal of character is an asset rather than a limitation in the form of comedy in which he exercises his dramatic art, because in the comedy of manners and morals the emphasis is placed on the brilliance of ironical social portraiture rather than on character. Certain types, therefore, appear again and again in Maugham's comedies.

One type is the elderly cynic, who appears as Paradine Fouldes in *Lady Frederick*, as Blenkinsop in *Mrs. Dot*, and as Champion-Cheney in *The Circle*. Of the society belle there are two distinct types: The more usual is that of the hard, cynical, and frivolous woman of the world, whether young or middle-aged, a type represented by Pearl (*Our Betters*), Rose (*Smith*), Lady Kitty (*The Circle*) (who, however, is only frivolous and foolish and not hard), and Lady Mereston (*Lady Frederick*). The other type of society belle, who, in spite of her extravagances, is at heart good-natured, is exemplified by Lady Frederick, Mrs. Worthley (*Mrs. Dot*), and Mrs. Wanley (*Jack Straw*). The young and ingenuous girl who is a foil to the hard society belle is another type, seen in Bessie Saunders (*Our Betters*) and Violet (*Caesar's Wife*). The "New Woman" is represented by Constance (*The Constant Wife*) and Penelope (*Penelope*). The young fop, a type reminiscent of Oscar Wilde, also appears frequently, as in Gerald Halstane (*Mrs. Dot*), Algernon Peppercorn (*Smith*), and Thornton Clay (*Our Betters*). Characters in Maugham's comedies, therefore, live only within the limits of the respective plays in which they appear, and there, again, they do not individually absorb too much

169

of our interest at the cost of the main purpose of the play, which is ironical social portraiture.)

Maugham's sense of the theater and his flawless dramatic technique combine with his attitude of ironic observation of life to excellent effect in his comedies, though, occasionally, his irony becomes cynical, and thus unpalatable. The place of the best of Maugham's comedies, like *The Circle* and *Penelope*, is therefore assured in the English comic tradition.

But the more serious of Maugham's plays do not succeed, for the technique which is so useful for the purpose of satirical comedy is hopelessly inadequate in dealing with themes which cry for a surrender to the emotions and a throwing of detachment to the winds. Hence, *East of Suez* turns out to be a meretricious melodrama full of odious characters; *Caesar's Wife*, a lifeless costume-play with wooden characters, fails to touch our hearts, for it has not touched the heart of its creator; *The Sacred Flame* misses the tragic note and becomes only a thriller; *Sheppey* only turns out to be a clumsy farce; *For Services Rendered*, a depressing play which even fails to satisfy the first test of a "good" play according to Maugham himself—the capacity to entertain.

Apart from the playwright's inability to grapple successfully with serious themes, his methods of pure objective portrayal of character are also, in a measure, responsible for the failure of these plays to reach a high standard of achievement. It is the lack of subtlety and depth in character portrayal that prevents a play like *The Sacred Flame* from attaining the true tragic note.

Maugham's Style

This discussion of Maugham's literary technique may be brought to a close with a study of Maugham's style. "We do not write as we want but as we can," wrote Maugham in *The*

Gentleman in the Parlour.[24] This wise observation is probably the outcome of Maugham's endeavor to formulate the right kind of style for himself, the story of which is told in *The Summing Up*. But Maugham's style shows the decision to write as he could, while at the same time writing in a manner best suited to his technique of the ironical and detached observer of life.

Maugham tells us that he is a "made" writer, on the analogy of the distinction between "made" singers and "natural" singers.[25] He had no regular training in the writing of English. So, "I have had," he says, "to teach myself . . . . It seems to me that I had a natural lucidity and a knack for writing easy dialogue."[26] For some time he followed models which were totally foreign to his temperament and capacities—Walter Pater, the Oscar Wilde of *Salome*, and Jeremy Taylor. But he soon turned to his right masters—Swift and Dryden—and played the "sedulous ape" to them. Maugham also names, in *The Summing Up*, Hazlitt and Newman as the two writers who have provided him with "a standard by which to test one's own style and an ideal which in one's modern way one can aim at."

It is interesting to note how Maugham's temperament, his outlook on life, and the peculiar technique which he developed all shaped the nature of his style. He had a matter-of-fact mind, more at home with the concrete than with the abstract, clear, precise, and with a strong logical sense, but one which was devoid of powerful imagination and of poetry. But he possessed, at the same time, an acute power of observation and a native gift of irony. By the peculiar accidents of his natural disability and his unhappy childhood and adolescence, he learned to suppress his sensibility quite early, developing instead an attitude of ironical indifference, for the expression of which he developed

24 Page 220.
25 *The Summing Up*, 55.
26 Ibid., 15.

171

the technique of the detached and satirical observer. All these factors have shaped his style. As John Brophy points out:

> The essence of his narrative style lies in his use of words not as instruments written and read but as instruments spoken and heard. He is less a writer than a talker—a view of him which is supported by the character of his prose and the construction of his novels and stories, and which is consonant with his success in the necessarily oral conventions of the theatre and cinema.[27]

This "talker's manner" was evidently necessitated by the adoption of the technique of the detached observer. This observer, while reporting his findings thought it convenient to adopt an easy, informal, chatty style in order to secure the attention of his audience. Simplicity, lucidity, and naturalness were indispensable for this "talker's manner"; mordant irony was a great asset, while elaborateness and complexity of sentence structure, subtlety either of thought or of expression, and all formal graces of style were to be carefully avoided as being unsuitable.

The strongest point of Maugham's style is its irony, sometimes biting and bitter as in the early passages describing the "popular" novelist Alroy Kear (*Cakes and Ale*), and sometimes playful and gentle as in the portraits of Elliott Templeton (*The Razor's Edge*), Captain Nichols (*The Narrow Corner*), Mrs. Albert Forrester ("The Creative Impulse"), and Bishop Blasco (*Catalina*).

Maugham's irony works by several devices: by the simple assertion of the exact opposite of what the author really means, as in the remark about Alroy Kear, "His career might well have served as a model for any young man entering upon the pursuit of literature";[28] by understatement, as in the description of the "mercy" of Bishop Blasco, the inquisitor—"Two or three fur-

[27] *Somerset Maugham*, 24.
[28] *Cakes and Ale*, 3.

ther instances may be given of his merciful disposition. Ever since the death of a penitent as the result of two hundred lashes, he had insisted on the scourging being limited to one hundred";[29] by exaggeration, as in the story "Louise" where Louise, the lady with a weak heart who might die any moment, "managed to go beautifully dressed to all the most lively parties, to gamble very heavily, to dance and even to flirt with tall slim young men," until George Hobhouse "had to brace himself now and then with a stiff drink for his day's work as Louise's second husband";[30] by paradox, as in the description of Mrs. Forrester's odes to the ocean—"she never again embarked on the treacherous element which she, however, sang in numbers both grave and sweet";[31] and by sudden anticlimax, as in the remark in *The Razor's Edge*—"Mrs. so and so would then tell me she had so much enjoyed my book, *Mr. Perrin and Mr. Traill*, and congratulate me on my play, *The Mollusc*. The first of these was written by Hugh Walpole and the second by Hubert Henry Davies."[32]

The limitations of Maugham's style are its almost total lack of poetry and of imaginative sweep, its poverty of subtlety and suggestions, and its excessive use of clichés and colloquialisms. The first limitation is well seen in Maugham's descriptions of places and persons. These are apt, short, workmanlike, but nothing more. Hence, the pictures of the "gorgeous East" in Maugham, though rich in external and objective detail, fail to catch the atmosphere of places, as those of Stevenson, Conrad, Melville, and Kipling always do. Consider, for example, the description of the beauty of the small Pacific island which, we are told, lured Edward Barnard away from civilization:

Below them coconut trees tumbled down steeply to the

[29] *Catalina*, 23.
[30] *The Complete Short Stories*, Vol. I, 440.
[31] *Ibid.*, Vol. II, 568.   [32] Page 7.

lagoon, and *the lagoon in the evening light had the colour tender and varied, of a dove's breast*. On a creek at a little distance, were the clustered huts of a native village, and towards the reef was a canoe, sharply silhouetted, in which were a couple of natives fishing. Then, beyond, you saw the vast calmness of the Pacific and twenty miles away, *airy and unsubstantial like the fabric of a poet's fancy, the unimaginable beauty* of the island which is called Murea. *It was all so lovely that Bateman stood abashed.*[33] (Italics are mine.)

We cannot share Bateman's emotions, however, for we are not quite convinced. The only approach to the truly imaginative in the whole description is made in the simile of the "dove's breast." Beyond that, the picture contains little: a few objective details; a very unsatisfactory comparison where the abstract is called upon to illustrate the concrete ("airy and unsubstantial like the fabric of a poet's fancy") in a pseudo-Shelleyan way, for the borrowed adjectives "airy" and "unsubstantial," now grown stale with use, are not quite helpful; the frank admission of defeat in the phrase "the unimaginable beauty of the island" which is a device to placate the reader; and the easy informality of "you saw" which seeks to indicate the narrator's meaning roughly to the reader—for that, and not a poetic piece of description, is the author's main aim in the passage.

Maugham's lack of imaginative power can again be illustrated by a study of the similes and metaphors used by him. These are seldom fresh, original, or striking. In the early part of his career, Maugham tried to enrich his style by working at poetic and picturesque similes and metaphors of which he gives certain examples in *A Writer's Notebook*:

> The rich death-colours of autumn were like an infinitely sad melody.

[33] *The Complete Short Stories.* Vol. I, 57.

The changing, rosy light of dawn.
The lamp flickered like the last wandering glance of a man
at the point of death.
The ardent, starlit night.[34]

But he soon gave up the misdirected effort and tried to cultivate
the qualities of "lucidity, simplicity and euphony." Maugham's
similes and metaphors generally seem to be flat and pedestrian,
quite serviceable to the "talker" for making his point clear by a
familiar image or comparison, but not powerful or rich enough
to illustrate, as by a sudden flash, the meaning of the writer:

> She hit on the commonplace *like a hammer driving a nail
> into the wall.* She plunged into the obvious *like a clown in a
> circus jumping through a hoop.*[35] (Italics are mine in this and
> the next two quotations.)

> The morning drew on and the sun touched the mist so that
> it shone whitely like *the ghost of snow on a dying star.*[36]

> Now and then a *sharp discord, like the scratching of a pencil
> on a slate, assaulted the nerves* with a sudden shock.[37]

This lack of poetry is most keenly felt in moments of
emotional stress in Maugham's narratives (and such moments
are not many), when he fails to move the reader. Two examples
of this may be recalled: One is the description of the illumination vouchsafed to Larry in *The Razor's Edge* (The passage has
already been referred to earlier [chap. vii].); the other is the
description of Bishop Blasco's eloquence in *Catalina*, which,
we are told, deeply moved the people but which fails to move
us because its description is couched in such journalese as "never
had he spoken with a more fiery eloquence nor with a more
heart-rending pathos."[38]

[34] Page 45.
[35] "Winter Cruise," *The Complete Short Stories*. Vol. III, 1348.
[36] *The Painted Veil*, 110.
[37] *The Narrow Corner*, 40.   [38] Page 131.

The inability to express subtle nuances of thought is inevitable in a style which puts a premium on directness and clarity at all costs. It is well seen in the passages which describe Larry's researches in Indian mysticism (*The Razor's Edge*) and in the account of Simon's political philosophy (*Christmas Holiday*).

But the greatest shortcoming of Maugham's style lies in its excessive use of colloquialisms and clichés. This shortcoming is inherent in Maugham's "talker's manner," for the detached observer must talk in an informal way. Hence, as noted by Brophy:

> Maugham is one of the very few contemporary serious writers to make colloquialisms the very substance of narrative. He does not reserve them—as, for example, Evelyn Waugh reserves them —for dialogue and quasi-reported speech, where they most economically and vividly establish scene, society, or period: nor does he use them as Henry James occasionally and surprisingly does, to throw a piercing side-light upon the characters.[39]

In Maugham, a person is always as clever as "a bagful of monkeys"; the beauty of the heroine always "takes your breath away"; a friend is always "a damn'd good sort"; the heart of a Maugham character always "beats nineteen to a dozen" in moments of emotional intensity; and a bore always "talks your head off"—and so on.

The persistent use of worn-out phrases and colloquialisms is fraught with great dangers. It is this that probably gives an air of cheapness to some of Maugham's works. But a greater danger is, as Brophy notes, that "nothing ages more quickly than . . . the 'apt phrases and picturesque idioms' of contemporary spoken language."[40] So long as they are used in dialogue, they serve admirably to vivify character and situation,

[39] *Somerset Maugham*, 22.
[40] *Ibid.*, 24.

but if incorporated into the narrative itself, they will within a few years turn the narrative into a period piece. Maugham's prose, one fears, may not escape this danger.

It is true that Maugham's progress from *Liza of Lambeth* to *Catalina* does show progress in the handling of words, though the progress is not in the direction of overcoming the limitations already noted, because these limitations are native to Maugham's capacities, personality, and technique. The progress is indicated by the fact that the prose of *Liza* and even of parts of *Of Human Bondage* is rather dry, drab, and rigid. But the prose of Maugham's later books has a greater suppleness, ease, and movement. Nevertheless, the crippling limitations of Maugham's style persist even in his most ambitious works, like *The Razor's Edge* and *Christmas Holiday*.

John Brophy perhaps goes too far when he asserts that, "Maugham . . . has never possessed the equipment necessary for a distinguished writer of prose."[41] With all the limitations of his style conceded, it would be unfair to deny the merits of lucidity, simplicity, directness, and euphony to Maugham's work when it is at its best. Maugham, as a stylist, lacks the vigor of Huxley, the subtle overtones of Charles Morgan, the imaginative sweep of D. H. Lawrence, and the delicate sensibility of Virginia Woolf. Nevertheless, the severe limitations under which Maugham's style labors are significant, for they are intimately connected with those of his outlook on life and his literary technique.

[41] *Ibid.*, 24.

CHAPTER TWELVE

Conclusion

·

T HE STUDY of the conflict in Maugham would be incom-
plete without a consideration of Maugham's defense of
himself against the charge of cynicism leveled at him. The defense is made chiefly in *The Summing Up,* though it appears
also, at lesser length, elsewhere in Maugham's work. In *The
Summing Up,* Maugham says:

> I have been called cynical. I have been accused of making men
> out worse than they are. I do not think I have done this. All I
> have done is to bring into prominence certain traits that many
> writers shut their eyes to. I think what has chiefly struck me in
> human beings is their lack of consistency. I have never seen
> people all of a piece. It has amazed me that the most incon-
> gruous traits should exist in the same person and for all that
> yield a plausible harmony. I have known crooks who have been
> capable of self-sacrifice, sneak-thieves who were sweet-natured,
> and harlots for whom it was a point of honour to give good
> value for money. The only explanation I can offer is that so
> instinctive is each one's conviction that he is unique in the
> world, and privileged, that he feels that, however wrong it might
> be for others, what he for his part does, if not natural and right,
> is at least venial. The contrast that I have found in people has
> interested me, but I do not think I have unduly emphasized it.
> The censure that has from time to time been passed on me is
> due perhaps to the fact that I have not expressly condemned
> what was bad in the characters of my invention and praised

what was good. It must be a fault in me that I am not gravely shocked at the sins of others unless they personally affect me and even when they do I have learnt at last generally to excuse them. It is meet not to expect too much of others. You should be grateful when they treat you well, but unperturbed when they treat you ill.

. . . I think I could be justly blamed if I saw only people's faults and were blind to their virtues. I am not conscious that this is the case. There is nothing more beautiful than goodness and it has pleased me very often to show how much of it there is in persons who by common standards would be relentlessly condemned. I have shown it because I have seen it. It has seemed to me sometimes to shine more brightly in them because it was surrounded by the darkness of sin. I take the goodness of the good for granted and I am amused when I discover their defects or their vices. I am touched when I see the goodness of the wicked and I am willing enough to shrug a tolerant shoulder at their wickedness. I am not my brother's keeper. I cannot bring myself to judge my fellows; I am content to observe them. My observation has led me to believe that, all in all, there is not so much difference between the good and the bad as the moralists would have us believe.[1]

In *Ashenden,* too, where the hero is, on Maugham's own avowal, a "flattering self-portrait,"[2] the charge of cynicism is answered as follows:

Ashenden admired goodness, but was not outraged by wickedness. People sometimes thought him heartless because he was more often interested in others than attached to them and even in the few to whom he was attached his eyes saw with equal clearness the merits and the defects. When he liked people it was not because he was blind to their faults, he did not mind their faults but accepted them with a tolerant shrug of the

1 Pages 38–39.
2 Page 197.

shoulders, or because he ascribed to them excellences that they did not possess.[3]

In the story "Sanatorium," where Ashenden once again appears as the narrator, there is yet another attempt at a defense: "People often said he [Ashenden] had a low opinion of human nature. It was because he did not always judge his fellows by the usual standards. He accepted, with a smile, a tear or a shrug of the shoulders, much that filled others with dismay."[4]

Similarly, in two of the rather cynical stories, "Virtue" and "The Back of Beyond," the narrator, when accused of being cynical, defends himself as follows: "If it's cynical to look truth in the face and exercise commonsense in the affairs of life, then certainly I'm a cynic."[5] And again:

> If to look truth in the face and not resent it when it is un-palatable, and take human nature as you find it, smiling when it is absurd and grieved without exaggeration when it is pitiful is to be cynical, then I suppose I'm a cynic. Mostly human nature is both absurd and pitiful, but if life has taught you tolerance you find in it more to smile at than to weep.[6]

The measure of truth in this defense has already been conceded in earlier chapters. It has been shown how the strain of human sympathy and sensibility is strong in the works of Maugham's first phase, and how there is a distinct note of mellowness and definite awareness of the major issues of life in the books of the last phase. Nevertheless, that there were certain distinctly cynical tendencies in Maugham and that these tendencies, on the whole, affected his work more strongly than the other strain, cannot be denied. From among the aspects of cynicism noted earlier in chapter one, there are few which can-

[3] Page 178.
[4] *The Complete Short Stories*, Vol. II, 917.
[5] *Ibid.*, Vol. II, 631.
[6] *Ibid.*, Vol. III, 1187.

not be detected in Somerset Maugham. Thus, the attitude and the technique of the detached observer watching life with ironical aloofness, which Maugham so assiduously cultivated, makes for a cynical lack of warmth in many of his books. The tendency to look upon morals and values with frigid indifference, originating in a conviction that all is vanity, also appears frequently in his work. It very often colors, as already shown, his attitude toward love; it is again illustrated in the philosophy of life which is put forth in *Of Human Bondage* and *The Summing Up*.

The negativeness of the creed in *Of Human Bondage* has already been commented upon in chapter four. There is a statement of Maugham's philosophy in the later pages of *The Summing Up*.[7] Maugham confesses, at the outset, that he has "no more special knowledge than can be acquired by any man who has lived for many years a busy and varied life."[8] But he tells us that he has "read pretty well all the most important works of the great classical philosophers .... Though there is in them a great deal that I did not understand, and perhaps I did not understand as much as I thought," and he adds, "I have read them with passionate interest."[9]

Maugham goes on to say how he lost his faith and how he came to look upon God "as a hypothesis that a reasonable man must reject."[10] Evil, according to Maugham, is an inexplicable problem, in spite of the theories which philosophers have put forth about it. Immortality, likewise, is a myth. His conclusion is that "there is no reason for life and life has no meaning."[11] Nevertheless, he has, he tells us, "sought to make a pattern" of his life. "But now if any one should ask me what is the use or

[7] Pages 160–212.
[8] *The Summing Up*, 161.
[9] *Ibid.*, 163.
[10] *Ibid.*, 171.
[11] *Ibid.*, 189.

sense of this pattern," he continues, "I should have to answer, none. It is merely something I have imposed on the senselessness of life because I am a novelist."[12]

The Summing Up was written in 1938, but in the preface to *The Partial View*, a one-volume reprint of *The Summing Up* and *A Writer's Notebook* (published in 1954), Maugham assures us, "I found that on the whole I had not much changed my mind on those great subjects of human meditation, the existence of God, immortality and the meaning and worth of life."[13] He confesses, in the same book, that he was for some time attracted towards Eastern mysticism, but had definitely rejected it.[14]

Even like its superficiality, the negativeness of Maugham's philosophy is self-evident. As R. H. Ward remarks:

> Maugham belongs to the transition from belief based on the findings of Darwin and Huxley, and those who made an "agnostic" of him (beliefs holding the material universe to be no more than material, a machine perceptible by the five senses), and the new set of values necessitated by the later findings of science, which reduce the universe to something strictly non-material. He perceives the new order but cannot so far free himself from the old.[15]

The Summing Up closes with a discussion of the three values—truth, beauty, and goodness. Of these three values Maugham thinks that "It appears impossible to say that either truth or beauty has intrinsic value."[16] He concludes by saying that "goodness is the only value that seems in this world of appearance to have any claim to be an end in itself."[17] But this

[12] *Ibid.*, 200.
[13] Page vii.
[14] *Ibid.*, p. xi.
[15] *William Somerset Maugham*, 202–203.
[16] Page 208.
[17] *Ibid.*, 210.

exaltation of goodness, one is tempted to say, appears to be little more than a rhetorical device, for Maugham has confessed earlier in *The Summing Up*:

> I have no natural trust in others. I am more inclined to expect them to do ill than to do good. This is the price one has to pay for having a sense of humour. A sense of humour leads you to take pleasure in the discrepancies of human nature; it leads you to mistrust great professions, and look for the unworthy motive that they conceal; the disparity between appearance and reality diverts you and you are apt when you cannot find it to create it. You tend to close your eyes to truth, beauty and goodness because they give no scope to your sense of the ridiculous.[18]

This is precisely what happens in Maugham's case, and, as pointed out earlier, most of the very few "good" characters in Maugham fail to succeed, while the obvious answer to Maugham's argument that he has always shown how much "good" there is in the so-called bad characters is that his "bad" characters are deliberately made agreeable, in order that their creator may have an opportunity to sneer at commonly accepted values. And how much of the sneering and captious faultfinding of the cynic is in Maugham is well illustrated in the long gallery of cynics, from Miss Ley to Machiavelli, who are the mouthpieces of the author in the books in which they figure. Maugham's admission, "I cannot bring myself to judge my fellows; I am content to observe them," is also highly significant. It is plain that this modest aim may easily degenerate into cold indifference to all issues. Maugham refers, time and again, to his "amused tolerance," but an entry in his *A Writer's Notebook* makes significant reading: "Tolerance is only another name for indifference,"[19] which, indeed, it frequently is for Maugham's "tolerance."

[18] *Ibid.*, 45.
[19] Page 31.

Moreover, as shown earlier, the cynical tendencies in Maugham appear to be the result of sentimentalism turning against itself—a process often seen at work in the genesis of cynicism. "If he [Maugham] has an affectation or mannerism," says Charles Morgan, "it is of ruthlessness. This is partly honesty and courage, but partly fear. Fear of what? Of sentimentality? Of being duped? Of self-deception?"[20]

H. E. Bates is even more explicit:

> Throughout Maugham's work and notably in the stories, there exists a pile of evidence to show that Maugham the cynic is in reality a tin-foil wrapping for Maugham the sentimentalist. Maugham's cynicism indeed peels off under too-close examination, thin, extraneous, tinny, revealing underneath a man who is afraid of trusting and finally of revealing his true emotions.[21]

The cynical tendencies in Maugham can be arranged in an ascending scale. First comes the studied indifference resulting from sentimentalism turning against itself, as in Miss Ley (*Mrs. Craddock*) who is Maugham's mouthpiece. This indifference soon leads to sneering and captious faultfinding, indicative of a denial of values as in the cynical obiter dicta in *The Moon and Sixpence* and *The Constant Wife*. The next stage is the deliberate boosting up of the "bad," as in the picture of love as mere lust, as in *Theatre*. Its corollary is the lukewarm nature of the admiration for the good—a point already illustrated in my analysis of Maugham's characters. And, lastly, we have the almost complete lack of idealism in Maugham's vision, as exemplified by his philosophy of life.

It is only Maugham's sensibility, which is strongest in his early phase and which continues occasionally to break through later, that saves him from becoming a cynic of the deepest dye.

[20] "Review of *A Writer's Notebook*," *The Spectator* (October 7, 1949), 468.
[21] *The Modern Short Story*, 145.

But the damage is done. Cynical tendencies have had their share in shaping Maugham's work.

The upshot of the conflict between Maugham's native humanitarian sympathy and the hard, cold indifference which he studiedly cultivated as a reaction has not, on the whole, been happy. The latter strain triumphed and became habitual; Maugham's achievement in his chosen fields of literary activity has consequently suffered to a large extent. The victory of the cynical strain in the middle phase of his career, when his art was achieving maturity, has condemned many of Maugham's novels to superficiality, lack of depth and of emotional warmth, and cheapness. These limitations are the more strongly felt when Maugham tries, in some of his later novels, to come to grips with the serious issues of life and the conflicts of the soul, and fails miserably and conclusively, because the attitude and technique of the detached, ironical observer are manifestly inadequate to handle those themes.

The fate of Maugham's humanitarian tendencies brings to mind the old story of the sword that rose and slew the slayer. Maugham had cut his fingers with the sword of irony so often that when he tried, towards the close of his career, to wield the august weapon with which alone the grim visage of life can be confronted, his fingers trembled, and the weapon turned back on him. It is only in *Of Human Bondage*, where his native sensibility has triumphed, and in *Cakes and Ale*, where the two strains in him have been perfectly balanced, that Maugham has been able to create something that will last, when *Theatre, The Painted Veil*, and even *The Razor's Edge* will perhaps have been forgotten.

Maugham's achievement in the field of the short story, too, has suffered. The many and much-publicized cynical stories, like "Rain," have given a bad name to Maugham's short stories, and created the impression that all his stories are marred by cheapness, superficiality, and an unpleasant lack of warmth.

Maugham's serious plays labor under the same limitations that mar his more ambitious novels, and again reveal the disastrous consequences of a habitually ironical attitude toward life and human character. These plays, too, miss their opportunities and fail decisively.

It is only in his "society comedies" that Maugham's cynical indifference produces the best results, as it is an attitude particularly suited to the conventions and the confessedly limited vision of the brilliantly artificial comedy of manners.

A couple of novels which escape, for one reason or other, the worst consequences of the attitude of "cynical indifference"; some short stories which reveal genuine sensibility; and a handful of "society comedies" in the traditional mold—that is all that can ultimately be shown to the credit of Maugham, while one feels the list would have been longer and richer, if the upshot of the conflict in him had been otherwise.

Cynicism is a disease to which the modern age is particularly susceptible. Ours is even more truly an

> *iron time*
> *of doubts, disputes, distractions, fears*

than was the age of Matthew Arnold. "When rule is gone from the commonwealth," observes Plato in *The Republic*, "chaos appears in the soul of man." Ours is such an age, an age of chaos in the soul of man. It is difficult to describe this chaos except in the illuminating words of Yeats:

> *Things fall apart; the centre cannot hold;*
> *Mere anarchy is loosed upon the world . . .*
> *The best lack all conviction, while the worst*
> *Are full of passionate intensity. . . .*
> *We are closed in, and the key is turned*
> *On our uncertainty.*

It is this "uncertainty" that is the keynote of modern life in all fields of human activity, whether material or spiritual. We seem to have lost our moorings in the welter of two world wars and all the destruction and disillusionment that they have brought; and the future looks bleak, with science frenziedly pursuing its mad career of annihilation. The very basic values have been threatened, and cynicism has, some time or other, laid siege to the heart of almost every major writer who has been Maugham's contemporary.

But it is significant that each of these contemporaries of Maugham—young and old—has fought cynicism on its own ground and has ultimately won over it, each in his own way, with his own weapons. Irony in Shaw and Samuel Butler did not degenerate into cynicism, for both Shaw and his master had a firm faith in the "Life Force." Galsworthy's so-called "dispassionate" observer of life—Cethru—could never be cynically indifferent, for his sense of pity was too deep to be suppressed; T. S. Eliot did not lose his way in the rocky, sterile "Waste Land," for the cool springs of religion did ultimately slake his thirst; Aldous Huxley leered cynically at life for long, but remained, at least for a time, to pray at the altar of Eastern mysticism. Even the studiedly neutral and antihuman amoralism of the young Hemingway turned in his later works into an all-embracing sympathy. The only major casualty was Maugham.

In the prime of his career, Maugham surrendered himself to cynicism. He stifled the humanitarian in himself quite early. He grew a thick skin; he learned to be on his guard against emotion, as well as against life and the world; he learned to be suspicious of the motives of men; he learned not to sympathize with or to blame men, but only to be amused at their foibles; he became a cynically indifferent spectator of life.

But this is not the way of the great writers of the world.

The great writers of the world have never been on their guard against life; they have never been frightened of emotion. They have felt passionately for mankind; they have praised and blamed men with great fervor; they have never been content merely with observing men coldly and indifferently; they have always plunged headlong into the struggles, great and small, of men; they have fought their battles, and they have lost and won. It is obvious that Maugham's place is not with them.

Maugham himself is much more modest and clear-sighted in assessing his own achievement than some of his fervent admirers. "I have no illusions about my literary position," he tells us in *The Summing Up*;[22] "This is slender baggage," he admits in *A Writer's Notebook*, "two or three plays and a dozen short stories, with which to set out on a journey to the future, but it is better than nothing."[23] Then again, "The greatest writers can see through a brick wall. My vision is not so penetrating";[24] and further, "so, never having felt some of the fundamental emotions of normal men, it is impossible that my work should have the intimacy, the broad human touch and the . . . serenity which the greatest writers alone can give."[25]

Maugham, too, could have given his work these qualities, for his equipment as a writer was admirable. He was a born storyteller, a keen judge of character, an able technician, and a shrewd observer of life with ample native sensibility. Travel furnished him with a vast and varied background. With all these advantages, Maugham developed merely into a very readable author, and little more. If tragedy is waste due to unrealized potentialities, Maugham's career may be given that name. One is tempted to describe his career almost as a tragedy with cynical indifference as the villain of the piece.

[22] Page 147.
[23] Page 338.
[24] Quoted by John Brophy in *Somerset Maugham*, 34.
[25] *The Summing Up*, 53.

The Terms "Cynicism" and "Humanitarianism"

.

Cynicism: The Oxford English Dictionary defines the word cynic as:

(I) One of the sect of philosophers in ancient Greece, founded by Antisthenes, a pupil of Socrates, who were marked by an ostentatious contempt for ease, wealth, and the enjoyments of life. (II) A person disposed to rail or find fault; now usually: one who shows a disposition to disbelieve in the sincerity or goodness of human motives or actions, and is wont to express this by sneers and sarcasms; a sneering fault-finder.[1]

The connection between these two (the ancient and the modern) definitions of the word "cynic" becomes apparent when one examines the doctrines, and the way of life preached and followed by the cynics of ancient Greece, who flourished for about a century after the death of Socrates. Antisthenes, the founder of the school, interpreted the Socratic dictum "Virtue is knowledge" in an extremely narrow sense: virtue as freedom from all wants, and knowledge as the sphere of practical action in individual life. These doctrines naturally led to a way of life in which the principle of individualism was carried to its logical extreme.

The cynic who existed for and in himself alone pursued the sole aim of self-knowledge and self-realization in conformity

[1] Vol. II, 1304.

with the dictates of his reason, ignoring the state and society altogether. Hence the famous words of Diogenes: "My aim in life is to deface the coinage"—the coinage of public opinion. The cynic's creed, when put into practice, became even more extremist, and it is not difficult to see the connection between the Greek cynic's egoistic individualism, his contempt for all human institutions and beliefs, and his rough frankness of speech and the definition of the cynic as a "sneering fault-finder" in modern English.

It is not easy to say when the transition from the ancient to the modern meaning of the word took place, though the process seems to have started, as Bertrand Russell suggests, in the very heyday of the cynic school.[2] The history of the usage in English of the words "cynic" and "cynicism," as given in *The Oxford English Dictionary* is illuminating. In the earliest example of the usage of the word in English, the word "cynic" seems to have been used purely in the ancient sense, as in Bauldwin: "He fel straight to the sect of the cinikes and became Diogenes scholar" (*A Treatise on Moral Philosophy*, 1547). Shakespeare and Milton also use the word purely in its ancient sense, as in "How vilely doth this cynic rhyme" (*Julius Caesar*, Act IV, scene 3, line 133) and "Men . . . that . . . fetch their precepts from the cynic tub" (*Comus*, lines 706–708) respectively. Curiously enough, it is Ben Jonson, with all his classical scholarship, who uses the word cynic in an almost modern sense in "Thou art such another cynique now, a man had need walke uprightly before thee" (*Every Man Out of His Humour*, Vol. II, chap. ii).

We could naturally expect the eighteenth century, "The Age of Reason," to be the first to use the word cynic in its truly modern sense. But *The Oxford English Dictionary* quotes only two examples of the use of the word from eighteenth century

[2] *History of Western Philosophy*, 256.

literature, and in neither does the word have any touch of its modern meaning.[3]

It is only in the nineteenth century that the word "cynic" appears to have been fully invested with its modern significance. Thus, William Alger in *The Solitudes of Nature and Man* (1866) describes the cynic as one "who admires and enjoys nothing, despises and conjures everything." Meredith observes in *The Egoist* (1879) that "cynics are only happy in making the world as barren to others as they have made it for themselves," and describes cynicism as "intellectual dandyism without the coxcomb's feathers." Oscar Wilde's brilliant epigram on the cynic is better known: "The cynic is a man who knows the price of everything, and the value of nothing."[4]

It may be noted, finally, how some modern writers define the word "Cynic." H. W. Fowler, in his analysis of cynicism, mentions "self-justification" as its motive, "Moral" as its province, the "exposure of nakedness" as its method, and "the respectable" as its audience.[5] Unfortunately, Fowler adds no comment on his analysis, which however could be interpreted as follows: The cynic's audience is the respectable, whom he shocks by his attitude towards life and morals; his province is morals, for it is towards the traditional values of life that the cynic is contemptuous; his method is "the exposure of nakedness," for he tries to strip values naked by sneering at them; and his motive is self-justification, for the cynic is a celf-centred individualist.

Charles Whibley, in his *Leslie Stephen Lecture* on Swift defines the cynic as: "One who looks upon life and morals with

[3] John Brown (1751), *Essays on the Characteristics of Shaftesbury* "All the old philosophers, from the elegant Plato . . . to the unbred cynic snarling in his tub"; and Cowper (1782), *The Progress of Error*, line 75—"Blame, cynic, if you can, quadrille or ball."
[4] *Lady Windermere's Fan*, Act III.
[5] *A Dictionary of Modern English Usage*, 240–41.

an indifferent curiosity, whose levity persuades him to smile upon the vices of others, and to let them go to destruction, each his own way."[6]

Desmond MacCarthy interprets cynicism as:

> Scepticism with regard to the depth and persistence of human affection, disillusionment with the excitements of passion, the conviction that men and women are competitive, ostentatious and selfish, and only superficially sympathetic, that time in the end gets the better of even those who are most intelligently selfish and a lack of faith in any cause of traditional morality.[7]

Humanitarianism: The term "Humanitarianism" has been defined in *The Oxford English Dictionary* as "the system, principles, or practice of humanitarians." Of the word "humanitarian" (sb) three distinct meanings have been cited.

> (I) Theological: (a) One who affirms the humanity (but denies the divinity) of Christ; (b) An anthropomorphite. (II) One who professes the "Religion of Humanity," holding that man's duty is chiefly or wholly comprised in the advancement of the welfare of the human race: applied to various schools of thought and practice ... (III) *One who advocates or practises humanity or humane action.*[8] [Italics are mine.]

["Humane" has been defined as "marked by sympathy with and consideration for, the needs and distresses of others; feeling or showing compassion and tenderness towards human beings and lower animals; kind, benevolent."] One who devotes himself to the welfare of mankind at large—a philanthropist. "Nearly always contemptuous" connotes one who goes to excess in his humane principles.

It must here be made perfectly clear that the term "human-

---

[6] *Literary Studies,* 355.
[7] *W. Somerset Maugham: An Appreciation,* 15.
[8] Volume V, 445.

itarianism" is employed in the present study in the third sense noted above, but without that touch of contempt with which it has been, as *The Oxford English Dictionary* points out, popularly associated. The term will be used here in the sense in which it is used in literature and literary criticism, when, for example, one speaks of the "humanitarian" strain in the work of Dickens and Galsworthy, referring to their sympathy for the "underdog," or of the "humanitarianism" of the Romantic poets like Blake and Burns, referring to their sense of pity for the lower animals, or again of the "humanitarianism" of Shakespeare, referring to the great catholicity of sympathy of that mastermind.

It is clear that in each of these three instances, the word "humanitarianism" is used not in the least in a pejorative, but on the other hand, in a definitely complimentary sense. In fact, the touch of contempt associated with the term "humanitarianism" in popular use can easily be explained as having been only due to the maudlin sentimentality and the indiscriminate philanthropy of which some of the humanitarians were, in actual life, guilty. It is in no way a reflection on the attitude of life called "humanitarianism" and the principles on which it rests.

The Autobiographical Works

•

I N HIS AUTOBIOGRAPHY, Chesterton speaks of "the morbid
and degrading task of telling the story of my life."[1] Maugham,
in his autobiographical works,[2] is evidently of the same mind,
because in the very opening sentence of *The Summing Up*, he
warns the reader: "This is not an autobiography nor is it a book
of recollections." A few pages later comes a stronger disclaimer:
"I have no desire to lay bare my heart, and I put limits to the
intimacy that I wish the reader to enter upon with me. There
are matters on which I am content to maintain my privacy. No
one can tell the whole truth about himself."[3]

The aim of *The Summing Up*, according to Maugham is:

> . . . to try to sort out my thoughts on the subjects that have
> chiefly interested me during the course of my life. But such
> conclusions as I have come to have drifted about my mind like
> the wreckage of a foundered ship on a restless sea. It has seemed
> to me that if I set them down in some sort of order I should see
> for myself more distinctly what they really were and so might
> get some kind of coherence into them.[4]

Again, "I write this book to disembarrass my soul of certain

[1] *The Autobiography of G. K. Chesterton*, 330.
[2] *The Summing Up* (1938); *A Writer's Notebook* (1949); *The Partial
View* (1954) [One-volume reprint of *The Summing Up* and *A Writer's Notebook*].
[3] Page 7.
[4] *Ibid.*, 5.

notions that have hovered about in it too long for my comfort."[5] This is apparently so important to Maugham that it makes him say, "I have long thought that it would exasperate me to die before I had written this book."[6]

This refusal to wear his heart on his sleeve is in keeping with Maugham's reticence and reserve which are English traits rather than French; though, as noted earlier, curiously enough, in his general outlook on the world and his literary technique, Maugham is more French than English. Its manifest lack of personal revelation, however, does not prevent *The Summing Up* from being an autobiography. For, in the larger sense of the term, an autobiography is, in the words of H. G. Wells, "the story of the contacts of a mind and a world."[7] Apart from this, contrary to Maugham's protestations, *The Summing Up* does tell us much about his life and upbringing, about the influences that have shaped his character, and about his development as a writer. An account of this has already been given in chapter ii.

Maugham has much to say about art, literature, and literary forms in *The Summing Up*. His approach to these problems is that of the competent [an adjective which he much resents] workman who knows his job and his tools thoroughly, and hence he has no high claims to make for his calling. In Maugham's eyes the artist is neither a prophet nor a savior; he is simply one who writes because he must. Maugham does not "believe that genius is an entirely different thing from talent."[8] His views on the nature and scope of certain forms of literature have, it will be recalled, been considered in chapter eleven, which examined his literary technique.

More than one quarter of *The Summing Up* is devoted to a discussion of philosophical questions. The limitations of

[5] *Ibid.*, 7.
[6] *Ibid.*, 6.
[7] *Experiments in Autobiography*, I, 28.
[8] Page 52.

Maugham's understanding of and approach to philosophical problems have already been indicated in chapter twelve ("Conclusion").

Lastly, *The Summing Up* attempts, as noted earlier, a remarkably sane and judicious evaluation, by Maugham, of his own literary achievement.[9]

Although English autobiography cannot boast of the unreserved emotional self-revelation of a Rousseau, it has a delightful variety of types to offer. Its many mansions include Cibber's chronicle of complacency, Watson's exercise in self-deception, Gibbon's even-tenored narrative of self-fulfillment, Mill's adventure of ideas, Trollope's manual of the craft of fiction, Mark Rutherford's drama of spiritual crisis, Wells's document of social change, W. H. Davies' annals of unspoiled ingenuity, Chesterton's paradox-studded world view, and Gosse's subtle unfolding of the process of the clash of temperaments, and sensitive records of the poetic soul as in the autobiographies of W. B. Yeats, Edwin Muir, and Herbert Read. Maugham's autobiography is obviously of a composite type; yet, as a self-portrait drawn, "warts and all," with the keenest observation and rare detachment, it is a valuable addition to the long line of English autobiographies.

The same spirit which makes Maugham say that *The Summing Up* is not an autobiography is seen behind his statement that his *A Writer's Notebook* does not "pretend to be a journal."[10] He evidently remembers the French writers of journals, a typical specimen of whom is André Gide who claims that a journal must not be "a literary restatement"[11] but a sincere and full statement of the writer's heart. Maugham meant his notebooks "to be a storehouse of materials for future

[9] Chap. xii.
[10] Page xi.
[11] *Journals of André Gide*, 26.

use and nothing else."[12] He has, therefore, not kept any record
of his meetings with interesting or famous people; and even the
jotting down of thoughts and emotions of a personal nature was
done "only with the intention of ascribing them sooner or later
to the creatures of my invention." His notebooks, the earliest of
which is dated 1892, amounted to fifteen volumes, which
Maugham has ultimately reduced to one.

A storehouse of literary material *A Writer's Notebook* indeed is. It is brimful with stories and raw material and with
lively portraits of men and women—specimens collected during
numerous travels. A short note of five lines written in 1902, for
instance, leads to the story "The Colonel's Lady," written
forty years later; and out of three notes written in 1916 came
that remarkable story called "Rain." Apart from this, certain
notes in themselves seem to make complete short stories—
dramatic situations with telling endings—as, for instance, the
note about a well-off woman who is miserable and does
not know why. She is "in search of her tragedy." She falls in
love and sees her lover killed before her eyes in an accident.
She becomes "happy," fat and contented. She had had her
tragedy.[13] Not all the raw material here has, however, been
tapped in Maugham's works. There are, for example, copious
notes made for a novel based on working-class life in Bermondsey—a novel which Maugham did not write because he found
later that life in Bermondsey had considerably changed since.

Many and various are the character sketches in *A Writer's
Notebook*. Though thumbnail sketches, each of them has a
clearness of outline and a finish about it. They include the
aesthete, the pedant, the poseur, the philanthropist, the planter,
the empire builder, the beachcomber, the hotel owner, the Jew,
the trader, the skipper, the secret agent, the swami and the fakir,

[12] *A Writer's Notebook*, xi.
[13] *Ibid.*, 267.

and a host of female characters ranging from the prostitute to the society belle.

Maugham's notebook also illustrates the development of his style, the story of which is told in *The Summing Up*. Thus, while the notes made in the 1890's abound in epigrams and in Maugham's exercises in opulent prose, the later notes show evidence of the lucid and limpid style of which the maturer Maugham became a master.

Obiter dicta on literary matters are naturally scattered through *A Writer's Notebook*. Some of these concern art and the artist, though on these Maugham has here nothing different to say from his views in *The Summing Up*. There is a spirited defense of the detective story, on which Maugham was to write a full-length essay later in *The Vagrant Mood*, and re-marks on individual authors like Jeremy Taylor, Arnold, Kip-ling, Dostoevski, Gorky, Turgenev, Chekhov, and Maupassant. It is an example both of the irony of circumstance and of Maugham's intellectual honesty that he allows to stand a note made in 1917, wherein Chekhov is hailed as "a spirit vastly to my liking," and Maupassant dismissed contemptuously as "a clever story-teller . . . but without much relation to life." A maturer Maugham realized where his true affinity lay. Apart from this, some of Maugham's comments reveal the happy knack of making a memorable summing up of an author, as for instance, in this note on Henry James: "In the end the point of Henry James is neither artistry nor his seriousness, but his personality, and this was curious and charming and a trifle absurd."[14]

Travel receives a fair share of attention in *A Writer's Note-book*. Here, as in the travel books, Maugham's eye for the graphic detail and his gift of ironical observation are revealed as, for instance, in the note describing his visit to the theater of

[14] *Ibid.*, 220.

Dionysus in Athens. A Greek student offered to recite something from the stage, and Maugham prepared himself "for a wonderful experience," only to hear the performer start, with an appalling accent: "*C'est nous les cadets de Gascogne.*"

There is not much of the social chronicle about *A Writer's Notebook*—the only two chief examples of which are: Maugham's account of his experiences as a doctor in France during World War I, which, V. S. Pritchett believes, "had it been expanded . . . could have been compared to Whitman's writings on the Civil War";[15] the narrative of Maugham's visit to Russia in 1917, wherein are vividly described the confusion and the turmoil of the early days of the Russian Revolution. Maugham's sympathetic but discerning analysis of the decay of France as a first-rate power; his praise for German habits of "industry and discipline"—praise given, too, at a time when it would have been "unpatriotic" to do so, viz., in 1941; his account of English reserve and modern American expansiveness and his attempt to explain this difference in terms of the admixture of continental blood in the make-up of the modern American—these, indeed, make one regret that so shrewd an observer as Maugham did not attempt anything of this kind on a larger scale.

Reflections on life and the world naturally abound in *A Writer's Notebook*. A reader familiar with *The Summing Up* will find very little that is new in Maugham's reflections on the problems of God and immortality, sin and morality, and other values. Stray reflections like the following reveal Maugham the realist and the ironic observer of human phenomena, sometimes approaching the borders of cynicism:

> I have never found that suffering improves the character. Its influence to refine and ennoble is a myth. The first effect of suffering is to make people narrow.

[15] Review of "A Writer's Notebook" in *The Author*, Vol. LX, No. 3.

There is one queer thing about patriotism: it is a sentiment that doesn't travel.

Commonsense appears to be only another name for the thoughtlessness of the unthinking. It is made up of the prejudices of childhood, the idiosyncrasies of individual character and the opinions of the newspapers.

One would have thought it easy to say thank you when someone has done you a service, and yet most people find it a difficult thing to say. I suppose because subconsciously their pride revolts at the notion that you have put them under an obligation. [This is pure Rochefaucauld!]

No journal writer, howsoever reticent he is, can avoid self-revelation. Maugham is no exception to this rule. One of the entries in his notebook reads, "Am I a minor poet that I should expose my bleeding vitals to the vulgar crowd?"[16] Yet there are less spectacular and unobtrusive ways in which one may reveal oneself. As in *The Summing Up*, Maugham does talk about himself time and again in his notebook, analyzing the make-up of his mind, dwelling on the influences that shaped it and on its limitations and excellences. He acknowledges his debt to France and French literature, in a note. Another note, with the autobiographical element in it thinly veiled, explains the causes of that fear of sentiment which is a curious characteristic of Maugham the writer: "He had had so little love when he was small that later it embarrassed him to be loved . . . and a manifestation of affection made him feel a fool."[17] Here are direct pieces of self-analysis:

My native gifts are not remarkable, but I have a certain force of character which has enabled me in a measure to supplement my deficiences. I have commonsense. Most people cannot see

[16] *A Writer's Notebook*, 41.
[17] *Ibid.*, 221.

anything, but I can see what is in front of my nose with extreme clearness.[18]

Again, "The turn of my mind is concrete and my intelligence moves inactively amongst abstractions."[19]

Of equal autobiographical interest are notes like the following, on certain landmarks in Maugham's career. Young Maugham's ambition and his sense of mission are revealed in:

> Sometimes I ask myself at night what I have done that day, what new thought or idea I have had, what particular emotion I have felt, what there has been to mark it off from its fellows; and too often it appears to me insignificant and useless.[20]

Similarly, "I was never without a sense of responsibility. To what? Well, I suppose to myself, and to such gifts as I had, desiring to make the most of them and of myself."[21] A note made immediately after his first taste of success as a playwright reads: "Success. I don't believe it has had any effect on me. . . . Its only net value to me is that it has freed me from financial uncertainties. . . . I don't think I'm so conceited as I was ten years ago."[22] There is also an interesting note on "middle age" and its advantages and disadvantages.[23]

Maugham's passion for irony makes him add, at times, comments on some of his early notes. Here we find a maturer Maugham turning the "oblique light" of his aloof and satirical observation against himself. In a weak moment, young Maugham has gone into ecstasies over "the feathery ball of the dandelion" which appeared to him to be a "a symbol of the life of man." An older Maugham pricks the bubble of romance with

[18] *Ibid.,* 122.
[19] *Ibid.,* 124.
[20] *Ibid.,* 53.
[21] *Ibid.,* 77.
[22] *Ibid.,* 69.
[23] *Ibid.,* 206–208.

a sly comment: "I didn't know then how succulent a salad can be made of this humble herb."[24] Another early note with a strong odor of sentimentalism about it, viz., "The autumn, too, has its flowers; but they are little loved and little praised," gets a strong rebuff later: "This is such nonsense that I cannot believe it was meant literally."[25] There are two striking examples of a change in Maugham's critical opinions. The early adverse note on Maupassant has been already noted.[26] Maugham's later comment reads: "In the above I was grossly unfair to Maupassant." The other instance is the disparaging note on Turgenev made in 1917, which "shows very poor judgment," as Maugham later adds.[27]

The journal has been put to diverse uses in different hands. To André Gide it is both a literary exercise, "a way of getting into the habit of writing," as well as an intimately personal document. Dostoevski's *Diary of a Writer* is, on the other hand, chiefly a crusade against social injustice. Henry James's notebooks are the record of a tormented artistic conscience; Hopkins' are a saga of aesthetic and religious fervor. The chief interest in the notebooks of both Virginia Woolf and Katherine Mansfield is the changing emotional climate in the minds of two gifted and extremely sensitive women. The parade of a worldly "ego" in Arnold Bennett has discovered a kindred spirit in James Agate. Hardy's notebooks are a medley of random jottings prompted by a lively curiosity; Butler's, a platform for the expression of opinion on topics ranging from art to science. When compared with all these, Maugham's notebook stands out for one chief peculiarity: its rich source of thumbnail character sketches.

In *The Summing Up* and *A Writer's Notebook*, Maugham

[24] *Ibid.*, 33.
[25] *Ibid.*, 47.
[26] See page 198.
[27] *A Writer's Notebook*, 134-36.

has made a distinctive contribution to one of the most interesting byways of literature. But to the student of Maugham's works, the two books are, primarily, valuable aids to the understanding of Maugham's literary personality. In spite of his avowals to the contrary, these pages throw a flood of light on William Somerset Maugham and tell us, "Behold the Man."

Maugham, the Essayist

.

ITH HIS LUCID STYLE, his polished irony, his supreme
readability, his wide experience of life and men, his
extensive reading, and his generally sound though limited taste,
Maugham was extremely well equipped for the role of an essayist. It is, therefore, a pity that he did not try his hand more
often at this literary form until by the very end of his career.[1]

Books and You, a long essay designed as the general
reader's guide to good reading in English and modern European
and American literature, was published in 1940. Maugham's
object in writing this essay was "to give to the general reader a
list of masterpieces which anyone interested in the things of
the spirit could read with pleasure and profit."[2] Maugham
speaks "not as a critic, nor as a writer by profession, but as the
plain man with a proper interest in humanity."[3]

His selection of masterpieces shows some curious features
which reveal his taste. Hardy among the novelists and Lamb
among the essayists are significant omissions; and in Henry
James, *The American* is preferred to the great novels of this
author's last phase. Drama is excluded altogether from the list,
except for a Shakespeare anthology, probably because prose

---

[1] *Books and You* (1940); *The Writer's Point of View* (1951); *The Vagrant Mood* (1952); *Ten Novels and Their Authors* (1954); *Points of View* (1958).
[2] Pages v–vi.
[3] Page vii.

drama is for Maugham "one of the lesser arts, like wood-carving."[4] But then, he has also admitted that poetic plays "have been preserved for the loveliness of their verse";[5] the reason for excluding these is not, therefore, very clear. Poetry is represented by two anthologies alone.

Certain tenets in Maugham's literary creed as revealed in the essay are: "Literature is an art. It is not politics, it is an art. And art is for delight."[6] The prime test of a book, often neglected by critics and professors of literature, is its "readability."[7]

Maugham's comments on books and writers are often shrewd and penetrating; for instance, in his summary of the characteristic features of English fiction, he says they are:

something robust, straight forward, humorous and healthy which . . . is representative of the race. There is no subtlety in them, and they are somewhat wanting in delicacy. It is a literature of men of action rather than of men of thought. There is a lot of commonsense about it, some sentimentality, and a great deal of humanity.[8]

Maugham is not hidebound to critical conventions, and there is a refreshing air of commonsense about many of his judgments. Thus, he can be bold enough to say, "The only thing that signifies to you in a book is what it means to you, and if your opinion is at variance with that of everyone else in the world, it is of no consequence."[9] He insists upon the reader's "right to skip," since, "to know how to skip is to know how to read with profit and pleasure," thought he admits that he himself is "a bad skipper."[10]

4 *The Collected Plays*, Vol. II, p. xviii.
5 *Ibid.*, Vol. I, p. xviii.
6 *Books and You*, 52.
7 *Ibid.*, viii.
8 *Ibid.*, 15–16.
9 *Ibid.*, ix.
10 *Ibid.*, 35–36.

There is a delightful piece of self-revelation in Maugham's statement that he finds it "more agreeable to read four or five books together"[11] according to his mood: in the morning, before work, a book of science or philosophy which requires a fresh and attentive brain; when work is done, history, essays, biography, criticism; a novel in the evening or a volume of poetry in case the mood comes up; and by bedside he keeps a book in which you can dip at any place and which you can stop reading anytime.

Memorable and trenchant critical comment is another outstanding feature, such as the description of Emerson as "a nimble skater who cuts elegant and complicated figures on a surface of frozen platitudes,"[12] and that of some modern prose as "hairy-chested, rough-neck prose."[13]

A passing glimpse of Maugham the ironical observer of human nature is also provided in the anecdote about a fair-haired lady whom he met on the Lake of Como. She always carried a volume of Emerson with her and heavily underlined passages in blue pencil—"perhaps to bring out the colour of her eyes"[14]—Maugham wryly observes. This lady who lives richly, still boasts about her "simple" life, and ultimately leaves her books to her gigolo!

Books and You is thus an extremely readable and generally sound piece of criticism and admirably fulfills the purpose for which it was designed.

The Writer's Point of View was the ninth annual lecture of the National Book League. Maugham's subject here is reading and writing, and the standpoint from which he views it is that of a writer of fiction. He does not agree that the main purpose of reading is to instruct; for him, it is to entertain. He

[11] *Ibid.*, 8.
[12] *Ibid.*, 63.
[13] *Ibid.*, 59.
[14] *Ibid.*, 61.

emphasizes "the admirable virtue of reading purely for pleasure without any ulterior motive. To acquire the habit of reading is to form for yourself a defense against most of the ills of life; it will enable you to bear a cold in the head with patience and the pangs of unrequited love with fortitude. But it is a habit that should be acquired early and no one is likely to acquire it unless the books that come to his hand afford him pleasure."[15] Maugham is aware that he will be branded as an escapist for saying so. His reply is, "all literature is escapist. In fact that is its charm."[16]

He thinks that the novelist is ill advised in being tempted to use the novel as a platform or a pulpit, since "if the novelist concerns himself with current affairs he runs the risk that when the affairs cease to be current his novel will cease to be readable."[17] The novelist may indeed deal with any subject under the sun, but he must not forget that the novel is a form of art and that the purpose of art is to please—the reading of a good novel being among the most intelligent pleasures that man can enjoy. The qualities of a good novel are "a coherent and probable story, a variety of plausible incidents, characters that are living and freshly observed and natural dialogue."[18] Maugham believes that the reader's understanding and appreciation of a novel are improved after knowing what sort of person the author is.

With regard to his second topic, writing, we have first, Maugham's memorable advice to the mother of a young would-be author: "Give your son a thousand dollars a year for five years and tell him to go to the devil."[19] The point behind the advice is that personality is the writer's stock-in-trade, and he

15 *The Writer's Point of View*, 8.
16 *Ibid.*, 9–10.
17 *Ibid.*, 11.
18 *Ibid.*, 12.
19 *Ibid.*, 16.

must cultivate it deliberately by exposing himself willingly to all the vicissitudes of life. The writer, according to Maugham, should be a man of extensive experience and wide reading and culture. He must also acquire the technique of the art of writing. This is not easy, because English, with its wayward grammar and enormous vocabulary is a difficult language to write.

The two principal ways of writing English are the plain and simple or the colored and flowery. Maugham's preference is for the former. His account of the history of English prose is that it was simple and plain until the sixteenth century, when for a variety of reasons, it became flowery and elaborate. Dryden restored the simplicity, and the plain style was brought to perfection by the writers of Queen Anne's reign, whom Maugham recommends as models to the modern writer.

Maugham concludes by saying, "it is an error to think the author's life is an easy one. It is a whole-time job. It needs industry, perseverance and infinite patience."[20] The only valid and sensible reason for adopting the profession of literature is "that you have so strong and urgent a desire to write that you cannot resist it."[21] The strength and urgency of a person's desire do not guarantee that he will write anything that is worth writing. Yet, he will have his own compensation: "In any case he will have enjoyed the intense pleasure of creation and fulfilled himself. He will lead a life of inexhaustible interest and enjoy as few can in this world of to-day, the inestimable pleasure of freedom."[22]

Maugham's views on reading and writing in *The Writer's Point of View* are identical with those found in his general critical theory as revealed in some of his essays.[23]

[20] *Ibid.*, 23.
[21] *Ibid.*, 23.
[22] *Ibid.*, 23.
[23] Essays on *Augustus, Zurbaran, The Decline and Fall of the Detective story, After Reading Burke, Reflections on a Certain Book,* and *Some Novelists I have known.*

Maugham, the Essayist

The Vagrant Mood is a collection of essays on various subjects ranging from the detective story to philosophy, and from
the life of an artist to a picture of late nineteenth-century manners. *Augustus*, the first of the essays, begins with a lively
description of a typical, small, country-house weekend during
the 1890's. Against the background of this quiet, leisurely life,
Maugham paints a rounded portrait of Augustus Hare, a minor
artist and writer of country guidebooks. In the account of
Augustus' childhood, Maugham's irony finds free play, especially in describing the experiments in self-denial which the
child was made to practice by his good mother, who intended him for the church. Later, Augustus' life as a country
gentleman is vividly portrayed. An acute analysis of Augustus'
character follows, his snobbery being illustrated through apt
anecdotes. (In fact, Maugham tells us that he once invented a
quip regarding Augustus' snobbery which has gained currency
as truth, and that he is writing this essay "partly to make
reparation to his memory."[24]) Augustus' horror of vulgarity, his
self-sufficiency, and his skill as a raconteur are effectively brought
out. One suspects that Augustus has perhaps provided the material for that finished portrait of a snob—Elliott Templeton—
in *The Razor's Edge*.

Maugham's interest is, again, mainly biographical in *Some
Novelists I have known*. Here are incisive sketches of Henry
James, H. G. Wells, Arnold Bennett, Elizabeth Russell, and
Mrs. Wharton. Maugham's eye for character, his mastery of
the vivid and apt anecdote, and his sense of dramatic situation
are all in evidence here. Thus, Henry James's snobbery and
pomposity and his agonized struggle for the right word in conversation; Wells' lively sense of humor and innate politeness;
Arnold Bennett's vanity, cocksureness, and worldliness; Elizabeth Russell's hard-boiled commonsense and charming malice;

24 *The Vagrant Mood*, 45.

and Mrs. Wharton's impossible perfection of good taste and good manners—are all neatly pinpointed. Maugham's comment upon Bennett's stammer is of special significance in view of the fact that he himself suffered from the same impediment during early years: "I think it is no small proof," observes Maugham, "of his (Bennett's) strong and sane character that notwithstanding this impediment he was able to retain his splendid balance and regard the normal life of man from a normal point of view."[25] One wishes one could say the same about Maugham.

In *After Reading Burke*, Maugham analyzes the texture and structure of Burke's style minutely bringing out its strong and weak points by illustration and critical comment. Competent as this analysis is, it is the presentation of the enigma of Burke's character—"He was upright and abject, straightforward and shifty, disinterested and corrupt"[26]—that remains the most absorbing part of the essay.

The Decline and Fall of the Detective Story is a comprehensive study of a form of fiction which has not received much critical attention. Maugham begins by distinguishing the detective story from the mere shocker, and thinks that writers of detective stories should be chary of their murders. He then analyzes the types of murders and murderers, the number of motives which actuate them, and the types of detectives. He admits humor into the detective story, though grudgingly, but firmly shuts the door to any love interest and fine writing. Next, the history of the form is traced, showing how the story of pure deduction has gone to seed and how it has now been replaced by the "hard-boiled" story of Dashiell Hammett and Raymond Chandler. But bad imitations have killed this new type also. There are shrewd critical comments: such as how the amateur

25 *Ibid.*, 233.
26 *Ibid.*, 141.

detective is specially popular in England, where the expert is always viewed with suspicion, and how the differences between the standards of personal cleanliness of the heroes of Dashiell Hammett and Raymond Chandler reflects the change in American habits over a certain number of years.

The essay on Zurbaran opens with an arresting account of a Spanish legend concerning the sanctuary of the Blessed Virgin near the Guadalupe River. The narrative of Zurbaran's life and career, to which this account is a prelude, is skilfully told, with a marshalling of interesting anecdotes. In assessing Zurbaran's achievement, Maugham seems less interested in Zurbaran the artist than in Zurbaran the man; thus, the most interesting problem about Zurbaran is for Maugham the paradox that "this laborious, honest, matter-of-fact man, should on a few occasions in his long life have been, none can tell why, so transported out of himself"[27] as to have painted, occasionally, pictures with a true mystic feeling.

Reflections on a Certain Book is an examination of Kant's aesthetics as revealed in the *Critique of the Power of Judgment.* Maugham's essay "does not pretend to be a philosophical dissertation but merely a discourse on a subject that happens to interest him.[28] This exposition of Kant's ideas is no doubt lucid —which can be said of few writers on the subject—but of greater interest to a student of Maugham would be his own ideas on aesthetics as given here. There is little, however, that is new in those ideas to one already familiar with Maugham's general critical position. As usual, Maugham maintains that pleasure is the only effect to be obtained from the consideration of a great work of art, that "the artist produces a work of art to exercise his creative faculty, and whether what he creates is beautiful is a fortuitous result in which he may well be uninterested,"[29] that

[27] *Ibid.,* 90.
[28] *Ibid.,* 175.

[29] *Ibid.,* 188.

self-expression is the sole aim of art, and not communication, which is accidental, and that, ultimately, "this gift you have of aesthetic appreciation has a moral effect on your character."[30] Each of these propositions is highly debatable, but perhaps, none more so than the last one, which might make the reader wonder where Maugham would stand if his own work were to be judged by this standard!

Here, as elsewhere, it is the biographical part of the essay which brings out, with playful irony, Kant's punctiliousness and his passion for punctuality that is most rewarding.

In *Ten Novels and Their Authors*,[31] Maugham discusses what according to him are the ten best novels in world literature, each essay being prefaced by an account of the life and character of the novelist in question. The introductory essay, *The Art of Fiction*, which sets forth Maugham's own theory of the novel has been considered earlier.[32] His remarks on the ten novels have nothing shatteringly original to offer by way of criticism. Further, significantly enough, Maugham seems to be more interested in the life and personality of each of these novelists than in the novels themselves. For instance, after devoting no less than twenty pages to an account of Melville's life and character, Maugham dismisses *Moby Dick* in five pages, of which three are spent in ridiculing allegorical interpretations of the novel. *Wuthering Heights* is slightly more fortunate in receiving ten pages out of a total of thirty allotted to it and its author.

Maugham's eye for character is seen to advantage in his analysis of the personality of each novelist. "With the exception

[30] *Ibid.*, 191.

[31] Essays on *The Art of Fiction*; Fielding and *Tom Jones*; Jane Austen and *Pride and Prejudice*; Stendhal and *Le Rouge et le Noir*; Balzac and *Le Père Goriot*; Dickens and *David Copperfield*; Flaubert and *Madame Bovary*; Melville and *Moby Dick*; Emily Brontë and *Wuthering Heights*; Dostoevski and *The Brothers Karamazov*; Tolstoy and *War and Peace*.

[32] Chap. xi.

of Jane Austen . . . in some respects all these writers were abnormal,"[33] he observes; and abnormalities of character have a
special appeal for Maugham, the keen student of human nature.
He brings out effectively the strange contradictions in Stendhal's
character, Balzac's garishness and worldliness, the profound
effect that physical disability had on Dostoevski and Flaubert,
and how the aged Tolstoy became the prisoner of his own mes-
sage. His analysis of repressed homosexuality in Emily Brontë
and Hermann Melville is a new and interesting approach which
could be very helpful in solving the riddle which the personality
of either novelist presents.

Points of View,[34] which Maugham announced as the last
book he would ever publish, is cosmopolitan in its range, with
essays on a German novelist, an Indian saint, an English divine,
and three French journalists. In his treatment of these subjects,
Maugham again showed a manifest interest in the man rather
than in his work. Thus, the essay on Goethe is entitled *The
Three Novels of a poet*. Although the novels are succinctly sum-
marized and intelligently commented upon, the most memorable part of the essay is the contrast drawn between Goethe the
man and Goethe the poet: "As a man he was selfish and self-
centred, stiff and unbending, impatient of criticism, with too
servile a respect for rank, and somewhat indifferent to the pain
he caused others . . . . He was his true self only when he wrote
poetry."[35]

In *Prose and Dr. Tillotson*, Maugham illustrates the truth
of the saying that "style is the man" with Tillotson's character,
career, and writings. He portrays the Archbishop, with a variety
of anecdotes and illustrations, as an upright, good-natured,
modest, patient, sincere, and charming man, and shows how the

[33] *Ten Novels and Their Authors*, 298–99.
[34] Essays on *The Three Novels of a Poet, The Saint, Prose and Dr.
Tillotson, The Short Story*, and *Three Journalists*.
[35] *Points of View*, 50.

simple, graceful and euphonious style in which Tillotson wrote was characteristic of the man. Maugham's views on prose style here are the same as those in *The Summing Up* and elsewhere. Of the two manners of writing English—the plain and the ornate—Maugham again characteristically prefers the former, as in *The Writer's Point of View.*

The Saint is a study of a different kind of man of God—a modern Hindu mystic. Maugham describes the life story of Ramana Maharshi as "strange and moving," and declares that he would tell it "as simply as I can, without comment or animadversion, without criticism of behaviour that to a western reader must appear extravagant; as naïvely, in short, as those old monks wrote the lives of famous saints."[36] Maugham's attitude to the Maharshi and his way of life is, however, obviously ambivalent. On the one hand, he gives an extremely clear and sympathetic account of certain tenets in Hindu philosophy; on the other, he describes ironically how the fact that he fainted while waiting to see the Maharshi was attributed, by people, to spirutual reasons, whereas it all happened due to a congenital irritability of the solar plexus in him! Maugham tells us, in *The Summing Up,* that he was once attracted towards Hindu philosophy—attracted enough, one recalls, to have been able to paint a superficially convincing pseudo-mystic like Larry in *The Razor's Edge.* But *The Saint* once again shows how Maugham, out of his depth in dealing with matters spiritual, must take refuge in noncommittal narration, sticking to the letter and missing the spirit.

In *Three Journalists,* Maugham has a subject after his heart: exercises in self-revelation by three French Journal-writers. He revels in this opportunity for analysis of character. The Goncourt brothers, with their overweening self-conceit and their genuine though misguided passion for art; Jules Renard, whose

[36] *Ibid.,* 61.

cynicism made him draw a brutally honest portrait of himself, but who was capable of genuine tenderness to his near and dear ones; and Paul Leautaud, a harsh, selfish, bitter man who hated men, but loved animals—all these men live in these pages, as they do in their own respective journals. Maugham's analysis of Renard's cynicism, the result of his being "a man warped by the unhappiness of his childhood, the hardship of his early life and a shyness that was almost pathological,"[37] should be of special interest to a student of Maugham, for, with certain changes, this description fits Maugham himself.

So pronounced is the biographical bias in *Points of View* that even in the essay *The Short Story* the lives and personalities of Chekhov and Katherine Mansfield receive as much attention as the theory of the short story, if not more. In his discussion of the form, Maugham adds nothing new to what he has said on the subject in the prefaces to his various collections of short stories and elsewhere. His portraits of Chekhov and Katherine Mansfield are, on the other hand, truly graphic, though he does not tell us anything about these two writers that we do not know from other sources.

Maugham's essays reveal a delightful variety and a wide range of subjects—biography, criticism covering several literatures and forms, and art criticism. Maugham the critic, whether of art or of literature, does not possess a highly original or penetrating mind. "Chekhov believed," says he, "what writers, being human, are very apt to believe, namely that what he was best able to do was the best thing to do."[38] Maugham's own criticism is not free from this charge. But his gift for trenchant comment and his lucid style make it highly readable. Generally speaking, Maugham's excursions into criticism reveal a mind with limited power of imagination, with little poetic sensibility, and with a

[37] *Ibid.*, 227.
[38] *Creatures of Circumstance*, 3.

rather narrow taste. It is a mind more at home with the concrete than with the abstract, more interested in human nature than in critical analysis.

It is, therefore, the biographical aspect of Maugham's themes which shows him in a better light. With his interest in human nature, his powers of observation, his realism, his polished irony, his flair for the incisive character sketch, and his narrative gift, Maugham was indeed equipped at many points for the role of a biographer. Hence, it is to be regretted that he did not try his hand at biography proper. But perhaps it is no mere accident that he did not do so, for the successful biographer is compelled to face life and human nature in the raw. This, Maugham, with his amused tolerance and cynical indifference, probably never could have done satisfactorily, as is clear from his own fiction. Interesting reading though they make, Maugham's essays are, therefore, apt ultimately to leave the discerning reader in the same disquieting frame of mind in which he finds himself after reading a typical Maugham novel.

Bibliography

Works by W. Somerset Maugham[1]

NOVELS

Liza of Lambeth (1897).
The Making of a Saint (1898).
The Hero (1901).
Mrs. Craddock (1902).
The Merry-Go-Round (1904).
The Bishop's Apron (1906).
The Explorer (1908).
The Magician (1908).
Of Human Bondage (1915).
The Moon and Sixpence (1919).

The Painted Veil (1925).
Cakes and Ale (1930).
The Narrow Corner (1932).
Theatre (1937).
Christmas Holiday (1939).
Up at the Villa (1941).
The Razor's Edge (1944).
Then and Now (1946).
Catalina (1948).

PLAYS

A Man of Honour (1903).
Lady Frederick (1912).
Jack Straw (1912).
Mrs. Dot (1912).
Penelope (1912).
The Explorer (1912).
The Tenth Man (1913).
Landed Gentry (1913).
Smith (1913).

The Land of Promise (1913).
The Unknown (1920).
The Circle (1921).
Caesar's Wife (1922).
East of Suez (1922).
Our Betters (1923).
Home and Beauty (1923).
The Unattainable (1923).
Loaves and Fishes (1924).

[1] The Collected Edition published by Messrs. Heinemann, London, has been used for purposes of making footnotes.

The Letter (1927).
The Constant Wife (1927).
The Sacred Flame (1928).
The Breadwinner (1930).

For Services Rendered (1932).
Sheppey (1933).
The Collected Plays. 3 vols.
(1952).

Collections of Short Stories

Orientations (1899).
The Trembling of a Leaf
(1921).
The Casuarina Tree (1926).
Ashenden (1928).
First Person Singular (1931).
Ah King (1933).

Cosmopolitans (1936).
The Mixture as Before (1940).
Creatures of Circumstance
(1947).
The Complete Short Stories.
3 vols. (1951).

Miscellaneous

The Land of the Blessed Virgin
(1905) (Travel).
On a Chinese Screen (1922)
(Travel).
The Gentleman in the Parlour
(1930) (Travel).
Don Fernando (1935) (Travel).
The Summing Up (1938)
(Autobiography).
A Writer's Notebook (1949)
(Belles-lettres).

The Vagrant Mood (1952)
(Essays).
The Partial View (1954) (A reprint of *The Summing Up*
and *A Writer's Notebook* in
one volume, with a new preface).
Ten Novels and their Authors
(1954) (Criticism).
Points of View (1958) (Essays).

Index

.

121, 123, 130–32, 134, 136, 156, 162, 170, 172–73, 201
Isherwood, Christopher: 93

Katha-Upanishad: 93
Kipling, Rudyard: 126

Lafayette, Madame de: 69
Lawrence, D. H.: 142–44, 151
Leverson, Ada: 16–17
Literary achievements of Maugham: 188, 196
Literary techniques of Maugham: 156, 160
Love: 152–53

Maugham, William Somerset: birth, 13; father, 13; maternal grandmother, 13; French influence on, 13, 25–27, 195; influence of disability and poor health on, 14–15, 18, 22–23, 47, 49, 51; life with uncle, 14; early school life, 14; death of mother, 15; year in Germany, 15; medical student in London, 15–16; Red Cross service in France during World War I, 17; marriage and divorce, 17, 151; daughter, 17; influence of travels on, 18–19, 23, 109, 132, 137–38, 188; World War II intelligence work, 19; stay in United States during World War II, 19; Order of Merit, 19; on the writer, 63; on middle-period plays, 66; reading habits, 206; on other writers, 209–10, 212–13
————, novels: *Cakes and Ale,* 14, 45, 72–83, 98, 107, 109, 116, 160, 162, 172, 185; *Of Human Bondage,* 14–15, 17, 29, 45–59, 61, 71–72, 74, 101, 115, 146, 148–49, 151, 159, 162–63, 177, 181, 185; *Liza of Lambeth,* 16, 28, 30–33, 37, 45, 79, 101–102, 109, 154, 159, 177; *The Moon and Sixpence,* 18, 24, 57–63, 71, 78, 81–82, 84, 107, 131, 159–60, 162, 184; *The Narrow*

Corner, 24, 83–90, 92, 138, 160, 162, 172; *The Painted Veil,* 24, 37, 63–66, 71–72, 80, 84, 92, 99, 123, 137, 141–42, 145, 149, 185; *Up at the Villa,* 24, 84, 99, 141–42, 160; *Mrs. Craddock,* 28–30, 33–39, 44–45, 64–65, 71–72, 79, 88, 92, 109, 148, 159, 184; *The Bishop's Apron,* 28, 44; *The Explorer,* 28; *The Making of a Saint,* 28–29, 44, 99; *The Hero,* 29, 44; *The Magician,* 29–30; *The Merry-Go-Round,* 29; *Theatre,* 37, 84, 99, 123, 141, 160, 184–85; *The Razor's Edge,* 80, 84, 89, 93–98, 106, 142, 148, 160–62, 172–73, 175–77, 185, 209, 214; *Catalina,* 84, 101–102, 105, 138, 142, 146, 160, 172–73, 175, 177; *Christmas Holiday,* 84, 89–93, 160, 176–77; *Then and Now,* 84, 99, 100–101, 105, 138, 141–42, 160
————, plays: *Lady Frederick,* 16, 39–41, 43–44, 168–69; *Caesar's Wife,* 24, 67, 69–70, 169–70; *East of Suez,* 24, 67, 69–70, 141–42, 145, 170; *Loaves and Fishes,* 28, 43, 53; *Jack Straw,* 39–41, 43, 168–69; *Mrs. Dot,* 39–40, 43, 169; *Penelope,* 39–41, 44, 67–68, 168–70; *Smith,* 39, 41–44, 67–68, 169; *The Land of Promise,* 39, 41–42, 44; *Landed Gentry,* 43; *The Tenth Man,* 43; *Our Betters,* 66–68, 167–69; *The Circle,* 66, 68, 72, 107, 147, 168–70; *The Constant Wife,* 66, 68–69, 72, 168–69, 184; *The Unknown,* 66–67, 70–71; *Home and Beauty,* 67, 71, 168; *The Unattainable,* 67, 71; *For Services Rendered,* 102–104, 149, 170; *Sheppey,* 102–105, 109, 162, 170; *The Breadwinner,* 102–103, 147; *The Sacred Flame,* 102, 104, 107, 147, 150, 168, 170
————, collections of short stories: *Ashenden,* 17, 110, 114–15, 118–19, 122, 161–62, 179–80; *Orientations,* 108–109, 111; *The Trembling of a Leaf,* 108–11, 117–18; *Ah King,*

W. Somerset Maugham has been cast on the Linotype in eleven-point Electra with two points of spacing between the lines. Foundry Deepdene was selected for display to complement the crisp, classic tone set by Electra.

The paper on which this book is printed bears the watermark of the University of Oklahoma Press and is designed for an effective life of at least three hundred years.

UNIVERSITY OF OKLAHOMA PRESS
Norman